THE ULTIMATE QUEST

Other Books by Don Fedor, PhD

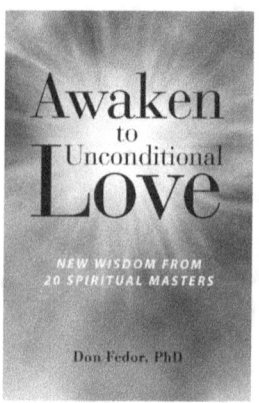

THE
ULTIMATE
QUEST

AWAKENING TO THE POWER OF LOVE

DON FEDOR, Ph.D

NAPLES, FL

Copyright © 2023 by Don Fedor

All rights reserved.

Published in the United States by
O'Leary Publishing
www.olearypublishing.com

The views, information, or opinions expressed in this book are solely those of the authors involved and do not necessarily represent those of O'Leary Publishing, LLC.

The author has made every effort possible to ensure the accuracy of the information presented in this book. However, the information herein is sold without warranty, either expressed or implied. Neither the author, publisher nor any dealer or distributor of this book will be held liable for any damages caused either directly or indirectly by the instructions or information contained in this book. You are encouraged to seek professional advice before taking any action mentioned herein.

All rights reserved. No part of this book may be reproduced or transmitted in any form by any means, electronic, mechanical, photocopy, recording, or other without the prior and express written permission except for brief cited quotes.

For information on getting permission for reprints and excerpts, contact O'Leary Publishing at admin@olearypublishing.com.

ISBN: 978-1-952491-43-6 (print)
ISBN: 978-1-952491-45-0 (ebook)
Library of Congress Control Number: 2022900984

Editing by Heather Davis Desrocher
Line Editing by Boris Boland
Proofreading Kat Langenheim
Cover and interior design by Jessica Angerstein

Printed in the United States of America

A significant portion of the book's proceeds will be donated to charity.

To the teachers,
mentors, and spiritual guides
who have come into my life –
often at the most unexpected times.

EVERYONE HAS A
QUEST

Contents

Preface – The Hero i

Introduction – The Quest 1

Author's Note 7

Year 1 The Knight and the Sword 9

Year 2 The Shield and the Stallion 33

Year 3 Starstruck and Stargate 83

Year 4 The Dragon and the Dark Night 153

Year 5 Love and the Quest 191

The Gifts of the Quest 221

The Key to the Quest 231

Acknowledgments 235

Footnotes 237

Readings and References 239

Book Group Discussion Questions 241

About the Author 243

PREFACE
The Hero

Throughout history, we have been intrigued with heroes and their quests – quests of discovery, quests to rescue others, or quests to right wrongs. From the vision quests of the ancient shamans, to medieval knights pursuing the Holy Grail, to more modern hero characters like Luke Skywalker, heroes and their quests are the foundations of enduring legends and blockbuster movies.

What is it about the hero that fascinates us? There are many answers to that question. Heroes make the difficult choice to leave their lives behind to face uncertainty and challenges. Will they have the fortitude to journey into dark places – both in the world and within themselves? Will they survive – and, if they do, will it have been worth it? Heroes often return from their quests to find the home of their past gone or their loved ones forever changed.

In the end, the hero's journey is about coming to "know thyself" more completely. The quest tests the hero – and in the process, the hero discovers more of their core being.

As we move through the quest, the metaphorical fires burn up all that is not who we truly are, so that what is left is authentic. We come to fully embody our true self.

Yes – each of us can be a hero, and our individual quests can take shape in unexpected ways. The miracle occurs when we have the courage to seek the truth that lies deep within us. And while a quest can challenge us, the gifts it bestows make it worth the journey. That is what happened to me, and that is what this book is about: *The Ultimate Quest* of the hero and the gifts bestowed by the quest.

Until you make the unconscious conscious,
it will direct your life and you will call it fate.

~ Carl Jung

INTRODUCTION
The Quest

The greatest quest we can undertake is not the battle with dragons out in the world – but the journey inward of self-discovery and spiritual growth. Our soul yearns to know the eternal truth about ourselves – to discover the treasure that lies within us – and to transcend our everyday lives while still functioning in the world. This unquenchable drive to know who and what we truly are has been a part of us since the dawn of humankind.

This book is the story of my Quest, and it is filled with events that blend the past and the present. It began in a way that I could not ignore; I believe it happened because – as with so many people – I was exploring beyond the boundaries of my normal life and career.

Some of my exploration was a result of life-altering events, like a significant bicycle accident I had in the mid-1970s. That crash led me to meditation, which helped me deal with some of the lingering effects of migraines. At other times, serendipity was at work –

such as when I discovered Edgar Cayce books while visiting a friend's house.

In the background of my normal life as a professor and academic researcher at Georgia Tech's business school, I felt that something kept pulling at me. It was a subtle but ever-present anxiety. I had a sense that there was much more to life – and to me – than what I consciously understood. I know now that it was the call of the Quest.

As I continued to cast my spiritual net, I discovered many realms. I meditated, worked with different mentors, attended workshops, and read spiritual books, all in the hope of bringing peace to my inner world. Because you are reading this book, I imagine you may have experienced something similar.

Although I had a number of ongoing spiritual practices, my Quest began in earnest during a workshop held in Winston-Salem, North Carolina. I had a powerful, surprising flashback, which shifted everything and led to a Quest of surprising dimensions. The many events of my Quest, while often challenging, gifted me with aspects of myself of which I was unaware. And the ensuing years included every conceivable emotion, from bliss to fear and everything in between.

While the events and hurdles in my Quest were specific to me, the overall nature of my journey will no doubt be familiar to you.

When I shared the story of my Quest with my publisher, April O'Leary, she asked a question that caused me to ponder my own motivation. She asked me why, with all of the challenges I faced, did I keep going on my spiritual journey? Why not simply retreat into my regular life, professional career, and outside activities?

The answers began with my Knight's appearance in the Winston-Salem, North Carolina workshop. His emergence ushered in an awareness of a greater purpose beyond what most people consider a successful life. The Knight also brought with him a steadfastness that was invaluable.

Another part of the answer is: heeding my desire for exploration did not always feel like a conscious choice. I was not constantly analyzing whether I wanted to continue. There was just that intangible something inside that kept me moving forward. Once I committed to the journey, there was no turning back. Even if I had taken a conscious hiatus, my guess is that something would have happened to draw me back.

To fully answer April's query, I must include the group of which I was a part for much of the journey.

There is a power in being in a like-minded group. For much of our time together there was support, encouragement, and a shared reality. These were the people to whom I could talk about my experiences – people who would not consider me crazy. Moreover, we believed we had come together to help each other, and possibly do something special.

The final part of the answer is that I wanted to know myself better, what I was here on earth to do, and to be more at peace. There had always been something gnawing at my insides. It was a sense that there was far more to this life than I could fathom. These are the reasons I continued on my multi-year Quest.

The Book That Insisted on Being Written

As you will see, this book is very revealing and shares aspects of my life that few people know. I was not planning to publish a book about my life – especially this particular portion of it – but everything changed some years ago when I was abruptly awakened in the middle of the night. At first, I thought maybe someone was breaking into the house or something had gone wrong – like my gas water heater exploding. However, my two dogs had not stirred, so something else was up.

As I tried to go back to sleep, I saw a vision that pictured a book index with the significant events that had taken place during my spiritual explorations. I assumed something or someone was telling me to one day write a book about my adventures – possibly during retirement when I would have more time. And, I thought, by the time I would start writing the book, I might have an understanding of where my journey was leading.

However, whoever or whatever had awakened me had other ideas. As sleep evaded me, the message was clear that I needed to get up and write down everything I had seen. I dutifully did so; and about an hour later, I put my notes aside. I was hoping sleep would return. As I lay in the dark, I committed to writing the book when I had time. But I received the message that someday was not the correct answer. I was to begin right away. While I tried to reason with my unseen visitor, explaining that I was already working far too many hours, it was to no avail. I finally acquiesced, and sleep was allowed to return.

Why was I commanded to write this book? The process of writing resulted in an expansion of my awareness and understanding of what had been occurring in my life. It began a more focused Quest – one I believe many of us share. It was, and still is, the journey of living unconditional love.

While what happened on my journey is unique to me, I suspect that much of what I encountered will sound and feel familiar to you. So, come, join me on the voyage of discovery that led me on the Ultimate Quest, and gifted me with priceless spiritual gifts.

AUTHOR'S NOTE

Italics – You will notice that there are sections in *italics*. Unlike the rest of the narrative in the past tense, these sections are written in the present tense. They indicate my experiences, and you are invited to join with me in experiencing these powerful events as I did.

Recall – Given this book was written retrospectively, the dialogue is as true to the actual conversation as I can recall. My hope is that it faithfully captures the essence of what was conveyed, even when it does not match the exact words.

Source/God – Throughout the book, I have chosen the word "Source" as a designation of the Supreme Being that represents love – unless I am using God in a historical context. I invite you to use whatever name, label or term is most comfortable. As the saying goes, a rose is still a rose, regardless of the name.

Names – Speaking of names, I have changed most individuals' names to protect their identities. Those who played roles in my journey have a right to their privacy, and can share their stories if they ever choose to do so.

YEAR ONE

The Knight and the Sword

Winter

A First Glimpse

On the journey of self-realization, we become aware that the reality in which we live is far more complex than it seems. We are not just physical beings who live for a time on the third planet from the sun. We are multidimensional beings. It is possible that we have had many "past" lives, and that we inhabit multiple planes of existence simultaneously.

Sometimes our first hint of this concept comes when we experience being in a new place – yet we know we have been there before (often called "déjà vu"). For example, a friend told me of touring Italy as a young man. As he walked the city of Pisa, he already knew his way around and never once had to open the map to go to the places in the "old section" he wanted to visit. Somehow, he just knew.

It is one thing to have an intellectual appreciation for how complex and multifaceted our lives might be – it is another to come face to face with that realization. For many years, I had entertained the idea – based on the work of people like Edgar Cayce – that we come in and out of the earth plane as we grow spiritually. And I enjoyed exploring that premise and other possibilities.

It is really something else to be transported to another realm and feel its reality. Dorothy and Toto, in *The Wizard of Oz,* suddenly discovered they were not in Kansas anymore. In their case, it was due to a tornado. We, too, can find ourselves in uncharted territory with our view of reality twisted in several directions at once. A tornado, of sorts, can show up in our lives when we least expect it. And this is where our story begins with yours truly – having my world turned upside down.

While I was living in Atlanta, Georgia, two events – one in North Carolina and the other in Toronto, Canada – changed my life's direction and set off a chain of occurrences. I was both shocked and gifted with a host of unexpected possibilities.

The North Carolina event was a weekend workshop designed to expand intuitive abilities. We were doing an exercise to help us become more sensitive to subtle energy. It was a straightforward activity – or so it seemed.

We each took a turn standing alone at the end of the conference room with our eyes closed, while the other participants – one at a time – walked toward us, circled behind us, and then retraced their steps to exit the room. Our job was to note if we felt drawn toward or repelled by each of them, and if we detected anything about them. The leader, David, held these types of workshops on a regular basis. He was considered an "intuitive" because of his ability to "get things" about people and situations without needing to ask.

After finishing my turn, I was proud that I could detect some differences, and I was excited to share my experience. When I approached David, who was standing in the doorway, he asked, "Don, what do you think of horses?" It was so confusing that at first I had no response. I am sure I looked utterly taken aback. Still bewildered by David's query, I answered that horses were big animals that I tended to avoid. His follow-up question was no less baffling: "What about a group of men?"

I am jerked back in time into a vivid "dream" that feels as real as anything I have ever experienced. Standing atop a gently sloping hill on a bright, sunny day, I am dressed in light chain mail armor, covered by a white tunic with a red cross embroidered onto its front and back. The chain mail is so well-fitted and familiar, it is part of me.

I am a knight on a battlefield. My senses are on full alert and I am ready for the fighting to come. In my hands, I am holding a gleaming sword polished to utter brilliance and honed to a razor's edge.

Scenes of death and chaos are unfolding around me. Cries from those engaged in combat and the screams of those wounded and dying envelop me from every direction. While out of sight, I sense that my fellow knights are off to my left, where the main battle is raging. I am on my own and I know it will be fatal. Even with sounds of fighting and suffering around me, within me there is complete calm.

I focus on the base of the hill upon which I am standing. A dozen men are charging up toward me. Dressed in simple garb, they are clutching knives and crudely fashioned spears. They are peasants pressed into service.

I drop into a defensive stance that requires no thought. It is pure instinct, having done it thousands of times in practice and on other battlefields. My right foot slides back; my sword shifts over to my right side, pointing skyward, as I lower my body into a semi-crouch. I am poised to engage the enemy. My next move will be a horizontal slicing motion in front of me from right to left at mid-chest height. The rest will depend upon how these ragtag soldiers respond.

Fighting a few of them would be easy. Fighting this many, I know the outcome. One of them will find an *opening. Watching them advance toward me, I know why I am by myself and allowing death to come. The killing feels utterly senseless, and inside of me is complete despair. As a warrior, I will now sacrifice myself in the only way I understand – to die in battle. A peaceful resolve descends on me as I await my fate, and the fate of those who will die with me.*

The scene evaporated from my consciousness. I looked back at David and he responded, "I thought so." He then turned his attention to another workshop member who was finishing the exercise. I stood off to the side, shaking, and feeling weak at the knees. I could not think straight. My emotions were bouncing all over the place. My heart pounded and I could not get my bearings. How did I go from our workshop to a battlefield and back in an instant, and how did David know where I was? The most important question, however, was, *Why is this happening?*

It was clearly me, in another time and place – but a different me. The battlefield was familiar, and my body reacted without conscious direction. Nothing in this lifetime prepared me to feel so calm or to have a sense of knowing about my impending death in battle.

If it had been a dream, the current me would have been scared to death and ready to run. For the rest of that day, I was in a complete mental fog. I remained quiet, trying to sort out reality from fiction. I know we did other things at the workshop that day, but they did not matter.

The next day, a fellow participant, Kimberly, sought me out. I knew her from a couple of previous workshops. She seemed far more advanced than I was when it came to things like intuition and psychic abilities. Although I did not really know her, I felt comfortable around her, and she was supportive of those who were less experienced.

Kimberly was the youngest in the group by at least 10 years, and she had a round, almost cherubic face. Her face matched her soft figure, which made her look even younger. The irony is that although she was short in stature, she had a commanding presence. When she shared her observations or assisted others, there was a mixture of power, wisdom and innocence. The gaze from her soft brown eyes went deeply into me – it was as if she could see my soul.

I discovered another surprise about Kimberly that weekend – what she did for a living. I would have thought that someone with her natural intuitive abilities might be an artist, or be in a field related to psychology, or possibly in a job working with children. I admit I was shocked when I found out she was an accountant who worked with small family-owned companies. She was a living reminder for me, not to make assumptions about people.

That day, Kimberly must have picked up on my confused and disoriented state, because she asked me how I was doing. I shared my "knight experience" with her. She listened intently and offered her insights. She said that what I experienced was a spontaneous past-life regression. According to her, it was during that particular "past" lifetime that I became disheartened with the church, the king, and God, and could no longer tolerate slaughter taking place in the name of righteousness. I ended that life feeling betrayed by the religious and political systems to which I had sworn loyalty, and disheartened by my belief that those I served demanded bloodshed for their own gain.

Her explanation fit the despondency that I could not shake. There was nothing left for my knight (me, at that time and place). All that he held sacred failed to provide a reason to continue the slaughter.

When I placed myself back in that battle scene, I knew there was no other option but to end my life in combat. I could not just walk away and say "enough." My

Knight's beliefs and his training led to the only exit he could accept. His values were deeply embedded, and I could sense that some of those values had followed me through time to my present life. Exactly what they were would be discovered later.

Why had such images shown up in this lifetime? I had no interest in knights, horses, swords, or chivalry. What transpired that day opened the door to events I could never have imagined in my wildest dreams. My Knight's abrupt appearance foreshadowed events that would challenge me on every level – and the next experience would not take long to show itself. The irony is that even getting to what came next would, in itself, prove to be a test.

Spring

The Coming of the Sword

I expected that after a mind-blowing experience, like finding myself on a medieval battlefield, my life would settle down some. I was wrong. As the saying goes, "Normal is simply a setting on the washing machine." Forget about "normal" when it comes to real life, especially when the door of a quest opens. There is no telling what will emerge. While I was still trying to make sense of the vision with my Knight, I discovered that his appearance was only the beginning.

Four months after the Knight appeared to me, I traveled to Canada for a follow-up workshop led by Shawn – who was a participant in David's workshop and a shaman in his own right. Shawn had spent years studying with a Hawaiian kahuna. He was leading a weekend of self-discovery and emotional healing at his home outside of Toronto. David and Kimberly (who had helped me begin to understand the appearance of my Knight) were both attending the workshop as well.

My flight was scheduled to leave on a Thursday and return on a Monday. Everything was fine when I arrived at the airport, but close to departure time, thunderstorms caused a delay. I boarded the plane an hour after the departure time, and I presumed that we were on our way. After taxiing out toward the runway, we halted for another line of storms. Even when the rain and lightning ceased, we remained parked. I thought we were waiting for our turn to move forward and take off.

Then the plane went dark, and the engines stopped. As we sat on the tarmac, the captain emerged from the cockpit holding a flashlight. He had a serious expression that did not bode well; he informed us that the plane had lost all electrical power. He was using backup emergency power to call for a tow back to the terminal.

In all my years of traveling, nothing like this had ever happened. While I had experienced everything from canceled flights, aborted takeoffs, nasty turbulence, and too many delays and rough landings to remember, I was dumbfounded about how a jet aircraft could lose all electrical power. I vacillated between thinking, *What the hell just happened?* to *Thank God this did not occur in the air.*

When I arrived back at the airline ticket counter, the representative informed me I was scheduled to fly out the next day. But after lots of pleading, she booked me on a flight to Toronto through Montreal later in the day. I called the group in Toronto and told them that although I would be arriving late that night, I would be there.

Or so I thought.

The flight to Montreal boarded as planned, but our departure time came and went. We continued to sit at the gate. A short while later, the captain informed us that our plane had a landing gear problem – another new flight experience for me. I could only resign myself to another delay. By the time we arrived in Montreal, the Toronto flight was long gone. It was time to find a hotel room for the night and reassess the situation in the morning. As I boarded a shuttle to the hotel, I thought about that next-day direct flight I had been offered and how I could have spent the night in my own bed.

Getting over my initial agitation, I did my best to take all of it in stride as a mere set of inconveniences. However, the group waiting for me in Toronto had other thoughts. They expressed concerns that there had been efforts to block my arrival. They could not offer much more, other than their sense that something was interfering with my journey. In their view, the multiple mechanical problems were not random coincidences. Since they could not tell me what was trying to prevent me from attending the workshop, there was nothing for me to do but deal with the immediate challenges.

I arrived the next afternoon to a warm welcome, and relief on the faces of my friends. The following day, we started to do self-exploration exercises in Shawn's furnished basement. There were two massage tables set up at opposite ends of the room. We took turns on the massage tables, where we were encouraged to go inward and bring up things that we felt were holding us back or causing us pain. While some of the participants really struggled, as evidenced by yelling and tears, I did not anticipate such hysterics for myself.

By midafternoon, it was my turn. I hopped up on the table and lay back for what I anticipated would be a pleasant exercise. To this day, it still amazes me how naïve I can be. Do you often experience this? I settled onto the massage table, face up, with my clothes on and my shoes off, and took a few deep breaths. Shawn was at my head acting as my guide, Kimberly was at my right, and David was at my left. Shawn instructed me to relax, breathe in peace, and exhale all tension and anxiety. I spent a few moments going inward, and then he said, "Envision a scene that will help you move forward in your life."

A scene arose.

I am standing on a beach looking out toward the ocean. The sea looks dark, angry, and uninviting.

Without leaving the scene before me, I gave voice to what I was experiencing. Somewhere on the edge of my consciousness, Shawn asked if I could move toward the water.

I wonder why I would want to do that. Even with that thought, I glide, dreamlike, to the water's edge. Looking up, there is a massive black wave looming over me, and I dive into it. The water churns above and I stay below the froth of swirling turbulence.

I described this scene and Shawn asked if I could breathe. I admitted that I did not know, but I was not drowning.

Everything feels OK, until I sense my spirit guide – a dolphin who appeared to me in a meditation some years back – pushing me toward the surface. What is this silly dolphin doing, propelling me up into the angry sea above? I have no wish to go there. I can sense the chaos. But her determination overpowers my reluctance as she drives us upward.

I emerge in the foam of a just-passed wave. The wave has crashed onto the beach and behind it the ocean is now smooth. My dolphin has disappeared; looking at the shore, I see a beach with dark volcanic-like sand. I move into the shallows, standing in the water up to my knees. Looking further inland, I see sand dunes and sea grass, but nothing else.

Before me materializes a prince, dressed in a formal white frock shirt and dark coat. The prince's serenity suggests a formal ceremony about to take place of which I am a part, despite our beach surroundings.

The prince is holding a sword out in front of him, and a brilliant light emanates from its entire length. It is pointing skyward and I have the overwhelming feeling that I am experiencing my own version of Alice's Wonderland.

The prince disappears – and just the sword is before me, suspended in midair.

I mentioned the sword and Shawn suggested that I take hold of it.

I extend my arms toward the sword, but my hands stop a foot away from either side of its handle. I have a deep sense of foreboding about taking hold of this powerful object. Despite my reservations, an irresistible force pulls my hands toward the handle. I try to hesitate, but my hands shift to right over left. I grasp the sword's handle.

There is a blinding flash of light, and it feels like a million volts of electricity slamming through my body. Every cell in me screams in concert with my lungs. Time stands still and my body shakes violently. The energy jolt subsides. Somehow

I have been transported to the water's edge, and I have the urge to put the sword's tip in the wet sand.

I lower the sword part of the way down, and another surge of energy courses through me. I hear myself screaming, as if disembodied, and feel more convulsions racking me. Gaining partial control over my breathing and racing heart, I bring the sword the rest of the way down so the tip of the blade is touching the mixture of sand and water.

My perception shifts back to my surroundings as I look toward the beach. A figure of light is coming toward me. It is Christ. He is not a man of flesh and blood, but the pure Christ of energy and consciousness. He stops a few feet before me. I recite a vow that emerges from deep within me and from long ago. It is the promise to use the sword for its truest purpose, even though I do not comprehend its implications.

Everything faded from view and I was aware once again of being on the massage table. My body continued to shake, and tears flowed down my cheeks. When the tremors subsided, I looked at Kimberly, who was on my right. She greeted me with a knowing smile, and said, "I was wondering when you'd take back your power." I lay there, trying to sort out my new reality.

Nothing in my spiritual explorations had prepared me for that, and even to this day I am still discovering the full meaning of her words. I could not dismiss the experience – the energy I experienced that day heralded the unfolding of my Knight's quest, a journey into unknown realms that would throw normalcy out of the proverbial window.

Vowing to use the sword for its highest purpose helped explain, at least partially, why my Knight gave up his life on that battlefield instead of continuing to take the lives of others. If he had taken a vow to use that energetic sword for "good," then slaughtering with its physical manifestation had to be tearing at his soul. The inner conflict must have risen to a level that was no longer tolerable, and so he gave up a role that was destroying him from the inside.

Meeting the Knight – who gave up his life and abandoned his quest – and receiving the powerful, otherworldly Sword were extraordinary events. Knights stand for strength and steadfastness. Swords, like the legendary Excalibur, symbolize a higher spiritual calling. Swords can also stand for destruction and bloodshed. These experiences called on me to grapple with my internal Knight's quest, and to decide whether I was willing to accept it. The Sword, with such incredible potential, challenged me to discover what I was supposed to do with it and whether I could handle its power. I knew that tremendous responsibility came with such power. My experiences also meant that I would be stepping further out of my normal life into a world of multidimensional uncertainty. The Knight and the Sword foreshadowed a journey into realms of myself that would challenge me on every level.

What I have come to appreciate is that symbols like the Knight and the Sword are common in the human experience. Many others have had amazing, life-altering events similar to mine. When we open ourselves to receive experiences that transcend our everyday lives, things will occur that change us and shift our beliefs about who we are and how the world works. While some of these experiences might not initially appear to be for the best, they are steps in our awakening.

YEAR ONE
Looking Back

Year One was a key turning point. To borrow a phrase, could I boldly go where I had never gone before? Or would I back away from what was occurring to preserve a semblance of normalcy? It was soon evident that the emergence of the Knight and the Sword opened a door to other realms of myself that I knew I could not close – regardless of where it led.

As incredible as the revelations were in Year One, I did my utmost to keep my spiritual journey and the rest of my life separate. I did not share my experiences with the Knight and the Sword with my professional colleagues or my students. Colleagues in my academic department knew I had a meditation practice, and that I attended workshops and went on retreats. When I was asked about those activities, I simply said that they were self-exploration experiences. If asked to explain, I would say something about getting to know myself better or dealing with childhood issues. Almost everyone could relate to those explanations.

At that time in my life, I was on my own and my main focus was on building my career. That included publishing my research in my field's major professional journals. I was also responsible for being an effective teacher, guiding my doctoral students, serving on academic committees (at least the ones I was unsuccessful in avoiding), and being a reviewer for academic journals. It was easy to become a workaholic, especially because of the time needed for research projects.

Outside of work, I had a furry companion, Fulton (a mixed terrier), and a house to maintain. What time I had left in my life I used for physical activity. When the weather cooperated, I would often go out on my bike.

There was, however, one significant overlap between my professional and spiritual worlds. It involved opening up to uncertainty. Doing so allowed the power of the Knight and the Sword to come into my life. When I first participated in the workshops, I had no idea where they might lead. Did I expect them to be so life-changing? Heck no – but I was grateful for what had occurred.

The same was true for my professional career. A few years earlier, I had grown tired of researching certain topics. Late one night, while working on a paper, I declared to no one in particular that I was finished initiating new studies in those areas. I made a commitment to make space for something new. Within a few weeks of my late-night proclamation, a colleague came into my office and asked if I would like to team up with him and a doctoral student on an organizational change project. The decision to say yes to that project altered the course of my work, and resulted in the most impactful research of my entire career.

While I was becoming more aware of the positive effects of opening myself up to change, there was one career area where I resisted doing so. It had to do with a promotion to full professor. For most academics, being named a full professor is a sought-after honor. I have known professors who became upset when they were told they had to wait for that status, because their record did not merit the step up.

So why did I not want that distinction? A promotion meant more exposure and more administrative duties – none of which I desired. I wanted to be left alone to do my teaching and research. Bottom line? I wanted to maintain my comfortable routine. However, my occupational status mattered to others in the college. So while my life was upended by my spiritual explorations, I was told my name would be put forward for a promotion – like it or not.

The irony was: as much as I was against taking the step, I was also unwilling to fail. If I had to go up for promotion, then damn it, I would succeed!

At the end of the year, I received a letter advising me I was promoted to full professor. I felt no joy; what I had done was simply to avoid failure.

In many ways, it did not make sense to dedicate my life to my career and then fight against recognition. Like almost everyone else, my responses to life are multidimensional and sometimes inconsistent. I could be attracted to new adventures – like the Year One workshops – and, at the same time, steadfastly hold on to established patterns.

Year One turned out to be the catalyst that opened up my life to many future adventures. The genie was out of the bottle – and there was no putting it back, even if I wanted to. The coming year was about to take me to places, especially within myself, that I would never have consciously chosen to go.

YEAR TWO

The Shield and the Stallion

Fall

Misunderstanding the Master

The appearance of the Knight and the Sword felt like they came with a requirement for me to step forward and be more conspicuous, something that always made me uncomfortable. I have avoided the spotlight, and I know that is a common response for many people. As I progressed on my Quest, I discovered a reason for my strong avoidance of the limelight – we come into this lifetime already holding fears from other experiences. We then manifest new experiences that confirm our aversion to being visible.

I discovered one key reason for this aversion at a mountaintop conference in North Carolina; it was a retreat that I had attended for many years. In Year Two of my Quest, the conference would play a key role in my Knight's quest and in my journey of self-discovery. At the conference, I had three poignant experiences.

The first was a past-life regression, reminiscent of what I experienced at David's workshop when the Knight appeared. However, this time, I knew the regression was coming. We began by closing our eyes, taking a few deep breaths, and relaxing. Our guide suggested that we recall a lifetime that could help us heal a current struggle.

I am with a group following Jesus. Hungry, unhappy, and exhausted from walking the entire day, I am frustrated because I do not know where or why we are going. I am traveling with this group because I committed to doing so. My faith is faltering, and my patience is wearing thin.

We are in a large grove of olive trees. The group of followers waits in the grove while Jesus goes off by himself to pray. It is turning dark; nightfall will be upon us in a few minutes. I slump against the closest tree to see if I can sleep. The tree is rough and uneven against my back and provides little comfort. This is our inn for the night. The prospects for food are bleak.

I am now at the crucifixion. Jesus is hanging from the cross and I am viewing His death from a hill some distance away. It is unbearable and I cannot fathom this sacrifice. Why has this happened? What is the purpose? We held such hope for the people of the world to embrace

Him as the one true spiritual light. His death is gut-wrenching and senseless. Here, the One, heralded as the Prince of Peace, is now dying a slow, agonizing death. Our efforts in the name of love are ending in nothing but suffering. Jesus is paying the ultimate price and our dreams are dying there with Him. Everything inside of me screams, "Failure!"

The scene before me changes again. I am in a small, dark, primitive prison cell, slumped against the outer wall. The wall is a rough texture of mud and brick, and above is a tiny window allowing a bit of light and air into my bleak cage. My body is depleted and dirty, and my depression is so deep that nothing matters. I have thrown my life away. The movement to bring love and compassion into the world has ended. I left my family to fend for themselves. I left a life of contentment and relative prosperity – for what?

I miss my small fishing boat and my life by the sea. I am dying for a lost cause. My family will never know what happened. I abandoned them and did not deserve their sorrow.

My perspective shifts to above my prison. Two guards carry my lifeless body out to a shallow grave and toss it in.

One of them remarks, "That's what comes from following a fanatic!"

Our leader called us back from our journeys. As I returned to my normal senses, I felt a strange mix of despondency and hope. I somehow knew the value of my time as a follower of Jesus; and, thanks to that experience, I better understood His message of love. We touched the hearts of many people and sparked a shift in consciousness for humans. That realization helped me to start healing the many feelings I carried from my former lifetime. It helped me to understand that I had avoided even positive notoriety because of the possible consequences. As a result of that past lifetime, being noticed for anything never felt safe in this lifetime.

As I sat there, swimming in a sea of emotions, it all made sense. Jesus received attention and adoration, which led to a brutal death, and what I perceived was a failure to bring love into the world. So, I took away from this that even if our intentions are to spread love, compassion, or hope, doing anything outside of the mainstream could be dangerous.

That past-life regression was another turning point in my Quest. It shed light on my difficulties with the biblical Jesus, who evoked strong – sometimes overwhelming

– feelings. It was easier to keep my distance, since it sometimes took every bit of my strength not to dissolve into tears when thinking of Him. This new discovery explained why I had a lifetime as a warrior Knight. From what I could tell, many of us have spent lifetimes trying to spread the message of love. When those lifetimes led to painful ends, we turned to the sword. But since that did not work out well either, we came to believe that there had to be another way. I was now given the opportunity to forge a path that would blend the steadfastness of the Knight with the love we learned from the Master.

Living on earth at this point in history is a special opportunity. We are here during a time of relative abundance and unprecedented tolerance for a diversity of spiritual perspectives. While intolerance and persecution exist, there may never have been another time in history with such a broad spectrum of religious thought. We are offered a chance to forge our own spiritual paths; we are fortunate to have wise teachers and circumstances to strengthen our spiritual wings.

Are we willing to use this freedom to its fullest? As the author Robert Heinlein suggested, our greatest gift is our freedom; yet, we often spend our entire lifetime trying to give it away. The answers many of us have been seeking are not "out there," but rather, within. I was beginning to awaken to these realizations through my Knight, who had returned to find what eluded him during his lifetime: the freedom to forge his own spiritual path.

The Sword's True Purpose

A large part of any quest involves releasing those things that hold us back. We cannot venture forward while being chained to our emotional baggage. My flashback to the time of Jesus helped me understand my struggles with Him in this lifetime so I could better embrace His message of love and compassion. The sword would play a staring role in what was to follow. The next regression-memory would show me that I needed to let go of fear and anger in order to move forward.

These emotions can be such a part of our lives that many of us do not realize that we are living with them as constant companions. We may be angry with how we were raised; how others have treated or abused us; the current struggles in our lives; our significant relationships (or lack thereof); our finances; or our inability to create a life that has meaning. Some of us feel the pain and suffering of the world or the crisis of our physical environment. There is no end to the things that upset us. And the one with whom we are often most angry is ourselves. So, what do we do with such anger?

In order to stay safe and be accepted by others, we have learned to swallow our emotional pain. We push it so deep inside that we do not even feel it, until someone or something comes along to trigger it. Then we have the opportunity to be upset with them – and with ourselves for being upset.

We who are on the "spiritual path" are often masters at hiding anger that we feel toward others and the world. We have encapsulated the anger so well that we not only fool everyone around us, but also ourselves. We strive to be Buddha-like and to desperately hold onto a veneer of calmness. We are the nice, compassionate types. "Who me, angry? Of course not; I am not angry. It is all those other people who are angry – but not me!"

At the same retreat where I experienced my regression as a follower of Jesus, I saw the angry part of myself in our second exercise. It was a guided meditation; we were to meet a guide to help us on our journeys. As we began, I found myself with my childhood pet, Snoopy, a mixed-breed spaniel. He had helped me through many rough times during my formative years.

Snoopy and I are walking through a flower-strewn meadow toward a mountain on the horizon. He is on my right side; and a woman, who feels like my energetic partner, is on my left. She is aglow with light, and her features appear ephemeral and fair. Her energy radiates glee, as if she is part pixie. We join hands and the three of us continue to walk the path together in sheer joy.

We approach the mountain, and the path turns to our right as it winds its way upward. Part of the way up, we come to the mouth of a dark cave. Standing at its entrance, I know it is my task to enter alone. My companions make no move to enter with me. (Thanks alot for the support!) While they wait outside, I go into the cave, which is about 30 feet deep. As I move halfway in, I see a ledge cut into the stone along the back wall. The ledge is four feet wide and three feet high. On the ledge is a plain chalice. Its simple form shows the marks of being handcrafted and is the only object on the ledge. Behind it, a feminine figure of light materializes – but says nothing.

I kneel in front of the chalice, and with extreme caution, reach for it. I do not know what to expect. Remembering what happened with the Sword, I am not inclined to rush. Taking hold of it, I lift the chalice and drink. There is no taste, but the sensation is of cool water to one who has a deep thirst. Something unidentifiable yet important is taking place. I replace the chalice with a sense of gratitude and reverence. As I look at the figure of light, she is even more aglow than when she first appeared.

I rise, nod to her in recognition and gratitude, and depart from the cave. Outside, the sun is vibrant, and my two patient traveling companions smile at my return.

Without a word, I am handed a sword and a shield, as if what took place in the cave affirmed my right to carry them. I sheath the sword between my shoulder blades and take hold of the shield with my left arm.

Snoopy, my female partner and I continue up the path of light-colored crushed stone, heading toward the mountain's summit. We have not gone far from the cave when a large, angry, black mass blocks our path. Its shape fluctuates as if it is flowing. I know this monstrosity is something from inside of me that does not want me to advance.

Fear envelops me as my mind races. This thing is massive. Fleeing in the opposite direction is a capital idea, but on some level I know it is not an option. How can I defeat this thing? It has no intention of letting us pass, and my companions are waiting for me to do something. Since this angry mass is of me, it is my problem.

I realize that the Sword is in my right hand. My adversary senses its energy, and gathers its strength to withstand a direct attack. Somewhere inside me, I know that attacking this thing as I would do on the battlefield is useless. Trying to hack away at this mass of energy, while appealing, is not a viable strategy. An awareness comes upon me that I should use the Sword for its true purpose. I somehow know, without a doubt, that this Sword channels love – period.

My adversary and I each stand our ground and I point the Sword toward the mass's center. A brilliant blue-white light surges out from the Sword. The ominous mass's outer edges change from black to gray, while its core stays ink black.

The Sword's energy continues to pour into the mass; little by little, it is transformed from black, to dark gray, to a light ash color, and then – nothingness. Relief washes over me.

We continue up the winding path to the summit. As we stand at the mountain's peak, the sun's brightness and warmth fill us with a joy beyond description. A spectacular lush valley spreads out below us and a river winds majestically through it.

I heard our session leader calling us back from our journeys. The scene faded, and I was back in the room with my fellow participants.

My experience was a glimpse of the role that fear and anger were playing in my life. These emotions were impeding progress on my Quest. Much of my spiritual Quest has focused on letting go of fear and transforming anger into love, but undoing many lifetimes of such emotions has taken years. The Sword has played a key role in my journey forward.

At the retreat in Canada, I began to understand why the Sword had come to me. Some months afterward, I remembered something Dan Millman said in his classic book, *Way of the Peaceful Warrior*. To him, the Sword can be an instrument of love that cuts away our illusions. Likewise, I hoped that the Sword would do exactly that in my life – lovingly cut away my illusions. My Quest had gifted me the knowledge of the Sword's true purpose.

Journeys of Light

Sometimes in life, it can feel like we are navigating a sea of uncertainty with a faulty compass and an inaccurate map. We set sail and think we are headed in the right direction – and then the weather conditions change, our ship runs aground, or we arrive at a completely different destination.

My Quest was teaching me that unexpected destinations can offer the greatest rewards, and adopting a sense of openness and wonder is invaluable. I was about to receive more gifts during that weekend at the mountain-top retreat.

Those gifts arrived during two experiences that derive from the spiritual practices of native peoples throughout

North America. The practices are known as shamanic journeys. A drumbeat is used to help one travel to the Upper World or Lower World. Traveling to the Upper World involves going out into space above the earth, where we often connect to our spirit guides. Journeying to the Lower World is going into the earth, where we find our animal guides.

It was at a previous shamanic-based workshop where I had met my animal guide, an exceedingly playful dolphin. I came to know her as D.D., short for Doris the Dolphin. D.D. and I had not connected in some time, and I was wondering whether she would make an appearance in my upcoming Lower World journey. It did not take long to discover that she was going to be my guide into both worlds.

My first journey was to the Upper World. Our leader instructed us to follow the drumbeat and to imagine ourselves moving out into space. Within moments, my journey began.

I am standing on a cliff outcropping, with my hands outstretched to the sky. I am an Indian chief, dressed in ceremonial attire of buckskin with fringe, and I am wearing a necklace of multicolored beads. My long, dark hair is shiny, as if oiled, and pulled back.

My mischievous dolphin comes from behind and shoots between my legs. I lock my legs around her and we head up through the sky. We ascend into the utter blackness of deep space and circle several planets. We break out into incredible light. Off to our right, two angelic beings are playing trumpet-shaped instruments.

As we move further through space, I see a magnificent castle in the distance ahead at the end of a valley. Its massive white blocks look to be of stone, but are translucent. It is not a typical castle, because it lacks any visible forms of defense. The main entrance and windows are open to the outside and brilliant light streams forth.

We drop into the valley and approach the castle. We enter, and move through a huge hallway. There is a throne at the far end. On the throne is a large, imposing male figure of brilliant white light – and, to his left is a smaller, female figure emanating a similar light. He reminds me of the god Poseidon in size and strength. She radiates a childlike essence in the body of a young woman.

D.D. and I stop in front of the throne. The imposing male informs me that the female light being is my partner. Hearing this, she jumps up with sheer delight, and runs toward me. Catching herself, she slows to a dignified walk. Bemused and enthralled at her approach, all I can do is smile. As our light bodies merge, I am overwhelmed with joy. Our combined light radiates throughout the castle and streams forth from every door and window, projecting out into the universe.

Together we get on D.D.'s back and head for home. We circle many planets, along with a few asteroids, to increase their light. I ask D.D. why we are doing the asteroids, since they are just large hunks of barren, lifeless rock hurtling through the blackness of space. She says that the light we give them will spread throughout the far reaches of creation.

Arriving back on earth, D.D. pulls up behind the rock ledge from where this journey began, and we step off her back. My partner and I stand, holding hands, looking out over the lands that stretch out before us. She shifts to standing in front of me and I encircle her in my arms. She fits perfectly. Her body presses up against mine and her warmth fills me.

Two young children, a boy and girl, come up from behind us and are giggling. They are freshly washed and dressed in buckskin outfits. I sense they are our children. I ponder having instant children, and I know nothing in this journey is logical. What part of riding on D.D.'s back through space, going to a light realm to find my partner, and coming back to our instant children is logical?

Both children look at me – and, with laughter in their voices, say in unison, "We told you so!" We all join hands *and follow a descending path to a lake. There is a cabin set back from the water's edge. We sit and watch the sunset while the children dance to a drumbeat. Realizing that the drumbeat is calling us back from our journey, I hesitate to leave this realm.*

As I opened my eyes, I found myself back in the room with the others. We spent a few minutes sharing our experiences. The smile that lingered from my journey seemed to encompass all of me. I longed to feel my partner's energy. That we might come together and do things to benefit the entire universe was beyond my dreams. Was it even possible?

The image that I could not fully grasp was the castle. Castles can symbolize anything from wealth and power to a strong foundation and protection. My journey's castle was different from the normal earthly ones. It was completely open and had no apparent forms of protection, such as a moat or other fortifications. It was also filled with light that streamed forth from within.

Most castles were dark and dreary inside, and openings to the outside world were intentionally kept small to reduce the castle's vulnerability. However, my castle was showing me the strength inherent in the light. When something or someone is filled with the light of love, it needs no external protection.

Our retreat group soon proceeded to the second journey – the Lower World. I was curious whether I would meet a new spirit guide – given that D.D. played a role in my journey to the Upper World – or if she might reappear.

I am on D.D.'s back (again) and we dive into the ocean. After entering a dark undersea tunnel, we surface in a pool within a small cave. The ceiling is about 10 feet high, and the entire pool is about 15 feet across. The dim light in the cave makes the still surface of the pool appear black as coal. Coming to the pool's edge, D.D. flips me off her back. She enjoys this little trick.

Mary, the mother of Jesus, is at the side of the pool, radiating an intense light that projects pure love. D.D. and I follow her up a path that takes us to a ledge overlooking Earth from the perspective of outer space. We watch as Earth's features change, the continents shift, and the oceans swirl. As this time-lapse picture unfolds, we see multitudes of souls leaving the planet. These departing souls appear as short lines of intense white light ascending from Earth's surface. I sense that in the coming years, a significant por-

tion of the planet's population may leave as Mother Earth goes through dramatic transformations.

Mary points out that from this vantage point, the changes are not frightening. They are simply what will be. We need not fear. I ask if I can help mankind. She answers yes – we will all be able to bring more light to the world and influence the extent and severity of the potential Earth changes. I feel hopeful that I might bring forth something positive to lessen the coming changes.

D.D. and I return to where the journey began – and, as the drumbeat is recalling us, she again tosses me off her back. I wonder why the jokes only go in one direction with my playful guide.

The second journey, while it was reassuring, also gave me pause. It pointed to major Earth changes and many souls leaving. How could my Knight, whose purpose was to protect and defend, help others during such a great transformation?

This last journey also suggested that changes would continue to come, and that some – at least on the surface – would be difficult. Time to fasten my seatbelt.

Throughout the experiences at the retreat, the opposing energies of love and fear were apparent. It became clear that every decision we make is a choice – to love or to fear. Many times, I acted out of fear – the fear of failure, the fear of being ridiculed, or the fear of being seen. Looking back on my life, much of what I had done was based on fear and its sidekick, avoidance. What I chose based on fear often led to anger and resentment, especially toward myself.

When I was able to make choices out of love – for example, helping someone – those choices brought joy and a greater sense of wholeness into my life. That awareness was a precious gift. I had been provided with a new way to view my future decisions and a way I might live my life more fully grounded in love.

Suppressed Memories

Kimberly had studied with a number of prominent healers and intuitives, and by now it was apparent that she was a gifted teacher. Belying her relative youth, she emerged as our group's spiritual mother, freely sharing her considerable intuitive gifts to help each of us progress. With our encouragement, she agreed to do a series of weekend workshops – and the first one would be at my home.

In her inaugural workshop, I was about to discover that a life I experienced as a military leader had been haunting my subconscious. Much of what had already arisen, specifically the Knight and the Sword, should have clued me that there was more to come – and that some of it might be overwhelming.

Preplanning

The day before the workshop, Kimberly told me that I would have a role to play in the upcoming weekend's activities. We sat at my kitchen table, and Kimberly sketched a picture of a six-sided, elongated figure that came to a point at each end.

Kimberly said that the figure represented the energy contained inside each one of us. This shape, an energetic crystal, rotates counterclockwise. She went on to describe a second energy field that surrounds the entire body. It is an egg-shaped aura that rotates clockwise, and extends six to eight inches above and below the person's head and feet. Each of us, she said, has a unique pattern in intensity and rotational speed of both the crystal and the aura. The combined pattern is like an energetic fingerprint.

Kimberly said that during the weekend, she would call upon me to work with each participant's crystal and auric energies. She described how I should visualize accelerating the internal crystal and then the external aura. Not fully understanding how that might be significant, I agreed to do my best.

Day One

In our first session of the day, we were releasing harmful beliefs, such as "I am not worthy of love," that are in our subconscious and difficult to access. We also did a release focused on forgiveness. Toward the end of that exercise, a shield appeared before me. There were not any particular emotions connected with it, nor did this shield seem to be the one I carried up the mountain back in the fall. It was more of an impression than a clear picture. I knew it was there, but it was on my visual periphery.

I did not give it much thought, but moments later, Kimberly announced a break. And when I mentioned my vision of the shield to another participant, a small wave of sorrow passed through me. Toward the end of our break, the sorrow deepened and I felt an emotional abyss opening. I knew I was in big trouble. I bolted for the garage and called out to Kimberly that I would join them as soon as I could. I was hoping to get into my car so I could sequester myself for what was coming without disrupting the others. It felt catastrophic. I could taste a mixture of fear, dread, and anxiety. My mind was scrambling around like a trapped animal, desperately trying to escape the inescapable. By the time I reached my car, I was sobbing. I slumped over the car's passenger side roof and let myself go.

I see a killing field and the bloody aftermath of a massive battle. Death and destruction stretch as far as I can see. The battlefield is a rolling plain of the dead and dying. I know I played a major role in this devastation – I thought this was God's will. Guilt pours from me. How could I believe this is what God wanted? How could I create such suffering? Wave after wave of remorse and self-recrimination slam through me as if I am being physically bludgeoned. Shaky and disoriented, I know this is a long-buried experience from which I had run away for lifetimes. The anguish it brings is smothering; and between sobs, I try to catch my breath.

Gaining a modicum of control, I sat in my car as a deep sorrow washed over me. My body was drained of energy, my nerves were shot, my heart was racing, my tears were flowing, and my head was swarming with battle images I did not know how to handle. Nothing in my present life had prepared me for what I was experiencing.

After a few minutes, one of the other workshop participants came to check on me. Through my tears, I shared what I had seen, and related my accompanying emotions of devastation and guilt. He reached into the car, put his hand on my shoulder, and told me he had seen a similar recurring scene his entire life. I could not have been more shocked. I would never have guessed that he too had such visions; but I took some comfort in not being the only one facing such memories. He soon headed back to the group to report on my frazzled condition.

More composed at that point, I moved upstairs to the guest bedroom and lay on the bed. Rejoining the group was not yet possible. Once again, the battlefield filled my vision.

I watch as the killing field transforms itself; the bodies fade, and in their place is a field of lush green grass and wildflowers. I am mesmerized by this shift – from what moments ago was a scene of horror, to where beauty abounds in its place.

I took this as a sign of healing, and felt my heart and emotions calming. A few moments later, I heard someone approaching the bedroom. As I opened my eyes, Sara came through the door. I knew her from a few earlier workshops; and while we got along well, I could not have guessed at the level of our connection.

I expected her to sit on the side of the bed and inquire about my condition. Instead, she dove onto the bed next to me, buried her face under my arm, and told me how much she loved me and that she was there to support me.

That added to my confusion – as if I was not already confused enough. What did this sudden show of affection mean? During the previous workshops we had attended together, I felt we were developing a friendship, but never anything more than that. As if to answer my question, a scene appeared in my mind.

Sara, as a young male, is up on a hillside above me working on my Sword. It is the same Sword I used when my Knight gave up his life. He (Sara) is getting the edge of the blade as sharp as possible, and I feel the larger truth. He is putting his energy into the Sword, lending it his strength. I know how desperately he wants the Sword to protect me.

I told Sara about my vision. I knew that the love she professed was from this other life we had shared, and a sense of calm knowingness came over me. Within moments, another scene appeared.

I am standing in an encampment with a group of other knights. Sara, as the young male, is on the rise above us. He is wearing a simple peasant tunic. While I am watching him, his tunic becomes a knight's regalia. As he descends toward the group, the knights spread out around me, forming a circle. They leave an opening for him to enter. Applause and cheers ring out as he joins us. Reaching me in the circle's center, we embrace, and I congratulate him on his knighthood. I am proud of myself for prevailing on his behalf, and proud of him for taking this step into knighthood.

When these mental pictures faded, I told Sara of the vision and how it felt. Through her tears, she smiled up at me and said, "I know this is true."

Wow – in a short period of time, I went from the depths of despair to seeing a light of hope about why these experiences were revealing themselves. We had been comrades in arms, and she had been there to support me as a knight. We were now back together to support each other on our journeys of rediscovery.

When we returned to the group upstairs, they were playing the game "Ask Me Anything." Kimberly used the game as a fun way to expand our intuition and our willingness to open ourselves to the group. The game used a child's toy wand that lit up with multicolored lights and made a whirring sound. The wand passed among the group.

As soon as Sara and I settled into our seats, the wand found its way to me. Someone asked, "So what happened?" Still embarrassed that I had lost all control, I looked to the group to confirm that they wanted to hear the entire story. What I received was a resounding, "Yes, of course," from everyone.

I told them what I experienced, and of the scene that had appeared before me. I admitted to feeling responsible for the devastation I had seen. The group asked me what sense I could make of the battlefield scene. I shared my desire that the path I was on would heal such experiences and would bring peace to me, as well as to all others involved. The image of the battlefields being transformed gave me hope that things were already shifting.

When I finished talking, Fulton, my mixed terrier, was sitting in front of me perfectly still – as if intent on hearing every detail. I asked him what he thought about all of this, not expecting any response. I was doing my best to inject a bit of levity into the situation. Kimberly piped up, "He is waiting for you to knight him."

Part of me wanted to run away from this knight stuff, but here was my faithful companion, stepping up to join the ranks. I was not sure whether to laugh or cry. Fulton broke the tension in the room, and everyone laughed at the improbability of knighting a dog – even one so regal. One thing was crystal-clear – no matter what I did in this life or other lifetimes, his loyalty would never waver.

I rose to my feet and stood in front of him. He did not move as I touched his head with the wand and knighted him: Sir Fulton. He seemed very pleased with himself, and his human could not have been more proud.

Day Two

I had been so immersed in the weekend's activities, and especially in my own revelations, that I forgot that Kimberly had a role for me. Alas, she remembered. Midway through our second day, Kimberly told me I would be working with the other members of our group following our lunch break. We reviewed what I should do – she reminded me of the shapes of the energy fields and how to work with each of them. I did my best to "see" what she was saying and to put aside my fears of inadequacy. Then, Kimberly called each person, one at a time, to stand at the opposite end of the room from me.

Closing my eyes, I begin. I envision the person's internal crystal spinning and then shift my focus to the external sphere. With both rotating in the proper directions, I turn my attention back to the internal crystal to increase its rotational speed. I sense I have done something similar to this in at least one other lifetime. There is a familiarity of working with others' energy structures.

After finishing with half the group, Kimberly asked me how I was doing. I admitted to feeling weak, but I wanted to work with one more person – Sara. She got up and walked to the other end of the room. Turning toward me, she gave me a loving smile and nodded to signal she was ready.

I envision her internal crystal and mentally spin it at a faster rate. Its light explodes, illuminating the crystal itself and projecting out into her entire energy field. Filled with boundless joy, I shift to her outer energy field – her auric energy – and encourage it to also rotate at a high speed.

As I opened my eyes, I saw a shocked look on Sara's face. She was feeling what I saw taking place. I stood there basking in glory; yet within moments, I felt light-headed. I plopped down in the nearest chair. I went from feeling proud of myself to feeling humbled. Kimberly took over and completed the group while I sat and tried to regain my bearings.

During the next break, David sought me out and explained why I had experienced the light-headedness. When I was doing the sacred geometry work, I used some of my own energy to power up the others, and therefore drained myself. While David appeared to enjoy my rookie mistake, he also advised me on how to more effectively channel Source's energy. He said I should take the highest point of light down through the top of my head, take it through my entire body to the center of the earth, and then bring the energy back up to my heart and project it out.

As a result of the weekend's experiences, I learned why my Knight disavowed his allegiance to all the authority figures he believed had commanded him to harm others. That disavowal was especially true for the ultimate authority – God. My knight had taken life in God's name and had suffered the consequences of feeling tortured inside. The Shield that ushered in those revelations was symbolic of my Knight attempting to protect himself from all that had caused him pain. To his dismay, his attempts failed.

Ultimately, our connection to Source is crucial to our spiritual quests. Rebuilding my own connection to Source turned out to be the most important first step on my personal spiritual path. The journey has encompassed many years. I did not know it at the time of that workshop, but this method of connecting with the Source of pure love would become the focus of my life and healing work.

The discoveries during that weekend led me to wonder: How many of us carry burdens from the past of which we are unaware? What do we have buried in our subconscious that needs to be healed and what experiences will help bring them into conscious awareness? This book opens with the quote by Carl Jung, "Until you make your unconscious conscious, it will direct you and **you will call it fate."** It is empowering to know that **fate** is often something that we can change.

LATE FALL

The Stallion Appears

At this point, my Quest was going full force, and I was trying to understand more fully the significance of the Knight, the Sword, and the Shield. But often, we are unable to recognize what is right in front of us – because, as humans, we have blinders to certain aspects of our lives. Those barriers are usually associated with fear. The challenge of overcoming that fear is where other people can help us. They can help us see what we are meant to do.

I received a clear reminder of how others can help in another workshop I attended, in the late fall. While I did not intend to do more workshops at that point since I had more than enough to handle at work, this one caught my attention. The topic was intuition – always an interest of mine – and it was to be conducted not far from my home. Moreover, it was only for one day. I felt called to attend it.

At the beginning of the workshop, while everyone was getting settled, I introduced myself to the woman sitting next to me, Amy. We exchanged our reasons for attending and I briefly shared my experiences with the Knight, the Sword and the Shield. I confessed my hope that the workshop would provide further insight into their appearances.

Our workshop leader, Linda, took us through several exercises to help open our intuitive abilities. She explained that our imagination is the pathway to our intuition. This turned out to provide invaluable guidance. It removed the pressure to be "right" – because there is no right or wrong when we use our imaginations. We often close ourselves off to subtle messages meant for us because we fear making a mistake. Linda suggested that we can receive messages as images, thoughts or impressions. Or, we might hear them, or simply have a sense of knowing.

For one exercise, we were put into pairs and I was partnered with Amy. We started the exercise by envisioning a door, and then opening it to see what was behind it.

I see a magnificent and massive white stallion. The imposing animal is standing in a majestic meadow of short grass and wildflowers with snow-capped mountains in the background, which I sense are the Swiss Alps. The stallion is rearing up and pawing the ground, appearing impatient and ready to go.

I suspected the stallion represented a part of me that was impatient to move forward, but as I was sharing that thought with Amy, she broke in with a question. "Isn't this your Knight's stallion; the one that goes with the Sword and Shield?" She explained how the stallion fit with my earlier experiences. It made complete sense – what was my resistance to putting these elements together? What was I afraid of seeing?

The revelations did not end there. A few nights later, following our one-day workshop, Amy told me she had the most vivid dream she had ever experienced. In her dream, she was in a movie theater. On the screen, a knight was riding in from the distance. At the bottom of the screen in large letters was the name Edward. The others in the theater were cheering and calling his name. She found herself transported into the scene and was standing in front of a crowd waiting at the village edge to greet this knight's return. The crowd was alive and filled with great anticipation as they cheered, "Edward, Edward!"

Amy told me she knew that I was the knight riding into the village, and that the people were cheering their champion and protector. In that lifetime, Amy and I were lovers and partners in the fullest sense, and she felt a deep sense of relief at her knight's (my) return. Her sense was that Edward spent most of his life traveling – our relationship was subordinate to his mission.

Amy also provided confirmation of the region I had seen during our workshop. In a phone conversation a week later, Amy told me she was not getting Switzerland as the location, but northern Italy. She was convinced I was mistaken. I asked her to pull out a world map. The part of Italy that she saw borders Switzerland. We both got a good laugh; we were seeing the same general location! Who knows where the national boundaries were back in those days?

I appreciated someone else confirming my vision. Frequently with such experiences, I would wonder if what I saw was only my imagination. How often do we receive something that looks and feels significant, but later discount it, because we convince ourselves it is all made up? Our rational side – the logical aspect of ourselves on which we have been trained to rely – can be uncomfortable with our intuition. Trying to reconcile these different aspects of ourselves can even make us question our own sanity.

It was clear – I was in the beginning stages of putting together the "what" and "why" of my Quest. While each experience was intriguing, it hinted at a much larger picture that was not yet fully in focus. The Knight, the Sword, the Shield, and now the Stallion were all pointing me in the direction of discovery and adventure. Each one had grabbed my attention in its own right. The question was, what did they foreshadow about my future?

Winter

The Gift

Up to this point on my journey of discovery, I had received a number of precious gifts in the form of experiences and insights. My Knight, the Sword, the Shield, and the Stallion were present in my life, because – on some level – I had asked for them. They were, as best as I could understand, guideposts on my Quest.

We each have incredible power to manifest things in our lives – often unconsciously. Messages, experiences, and objects frequently show up unexpectedly, and in ways we could not previously imagine. The surprise element happens because we are creating from the subconscious level. Sometimes we create experiences, as I did. At other times, material objects come to us unexpectedly. That was what happened to me next.

Kimberly, our teacher and mentor, was in a transition period in her life, so I offered her my guest bedroom. She appreciated having a way station, and I enjoyed having her company. Moreover, she took care of Sir Fulton when I needed to travel. Because we both had active travel schedules, we never tired of each other. As Christmas approached, my year-end work and my Christmas gift list kept me busy. While the Yuletide season is one of my favorite times of the year, the season's "To-Do List" can be daunting

One afternoon in mid-December, a large and cumbersome package arrived for Kimberly. Not giving it much thought, except that she might have trouble lifting the darn thing, I moved it into her room. I could not imagine what it could contain with such heft and size. That evening, when she called from her work site in Texas, I mentioned her package. To my surprise, she said with glee, "That's your gift!" I was baffled as to what it could be; but it reminded me that I did not yet have a gift for her, and so I added that to my "To-Do List."

When Kimberly arrived back at the house a week later, she dragged – and I mean dragged – the box out into the living room. She announced that it was time for me to open my gift. Since I am better at giving than receiving, I suggested we wait until my return from spending the holidays with my family. I did not want to admit that I was reluctant to see what was inside the box.

Bless her pushy little soul, Kimberly was having none of my delay tactics. She insisted that now was the right time. I pried open the box to find a sword – a replica of Excalibur, measuring 4 feet long and 7 inches across at the guard. It was a massive weapon, decorated with simulated gold and colorful gems on the guard and handle.

I stood there, speechless. My first thought was, *Can we send this back?* The sword was ornate to the extreme. The sword that went with my Knight into battle was similar in mass to this one, but was devoid of jewels. While this object was a work of art, my Knight valued functionality – a sword was meant to be effective as a weapon.

Why was this particular sword coming into my life? I felt torn between telling her, "Thanks, but no thanks," and the desire to not hurt her feelings. Kimberly was obviously excited about this gift, and it was apparent that she believed she was doing something special.

She waited for me to say something – and when I did not, she asked, "Well, what do you think?" Caught off guard, I stammered about how amazing it was and bent to pick it up. Although heavy, it felt natural in my hands, and I could feel it transporting me to another time and place. Again, Kimberly broke through, and asked, "Is it messing with you?"

Yes, it sure was. Never in my wildest dreams did I expect to hold such a sword. Maybe, I thought, it was a ceremonial sword that held a yet-to-be-revealed significance. This one, thankfully, came without a wallop of energy like the one in my past-life experience.

Over the next year and a half, the sword and I worked together to forge a connection. I practiced different movements that felt familiar from ages ago. But one evening, while I was practicing with the sword inside my home, everything changed. I felt the urge to kneel down on one knee, place the sword in front of me with the tip resting on the carpet and the handle pointed straight upward. My hands rested on the guard on either side of the handle. As I relaxed into this pose – a pose that felt all too familiar – a scene appeared.

It is a few hours before dawn. I am overlooking a field where a battle will take place. In the pre-battle stillness, I wait with reverent anticipation.

The scene vanished. I remained in my kneeling position and contemplated what the vision might mean. Unlike in the days when my Knight lived, I understood that there would not be any battles or slaughter with this sword. I knew that this particular energetic sword channeled only love – as I was shown in my vision-journey up the mountain when I faced my fear with Snoopy and my female companion.

Later that evening, I lay in bed with the sword next to me. My eyes were closed. As if to confirm my belief about the sword, I had another transforming vision.

I reach out and take hold of the sword's handle. Within moments, my hand is pulsing with waves of energy. I maintain my hold for a few minutes and as the feeling subsides, I sense that I should hold my hand just above the handle. The palm of my hand is hot. I am confused as to what is taking place, but I sense this Sword's power as an instrument of love.

Love, and its incredible power, continued to manifest in my life. At each turn in my Quest, it was the one constant calling me to continue. After my experiences with the new sword, I would often ponder what I was meant to do with such power and what it would mean for my life.

YEAR TWO
Looking Back

When I opened the door to the Knight and the Sword, I could never have predicted that so much would happen in Year Two. I gained a greater understanding of my fear of being visible or noticed, the anger I was unconsciously harboring, and the incredible power of love.

I was also being schooled in the nature of loss. Two family members – my brother-in-law and my Dad – departed from the earth via death. My brother-in-law died unexpectedly at 61, but my dad had been on hospice – so, his death was long-anticipated. Each loss evoked different feelings within me – and yet, in the end, each loss needed to be accepted. One of them nudged me toward merging my worlds.

Up to this point, I maintained a solid barrier between my spiritual explorations and the rest of my life. I believed that my colleagues, friends and family did not need to know what I was doing or experiencing in the spiritual realm. However, early in Year Two, that belief was challenged, and I was shown the possible benefits of selectively letting down the barrier.

While Mom and Dad had remained in Florida because Dad was under hospice care, the rest of the family gathered up in the Northeast to attend the memorial service for my brother-in-law. I believe we were all vacillating between denial and shock. People in our family tended to live into their 90s. Losing my brother-in-law at such a young age simply did not make sense.

On the morning of the memorial service, there was a light knock on my bedroom door. It was my brother, Allen. He came to inform me that Dad had died the night before. Mom had called Allen's cell phone about an hour earlier, but he had waited to tell me, wanting to allow me to sleep.

Allen pulled up a chair at the end of my bed and we began to share our views of death. I decided to tell him about my experiences that had led me to believe that life on earth was not a "one-and-done" situation. I knew it was a risk, but what happened afterward showed me that the risk was worth it.

He told me that there was something he had never shared with anyone before, for fear of appearing delusional. Leaning forward and looking serious, he began. When he was about 6 years old, he had a dream. More accurately, it was a lucid nightmare. He was the pilot of a World War II B-25 bomber. The aircraft was in flames, and he was doing his best to control it so the crew could bail out. Then, he planned to jump.

From what my brother told me, he was not just dreaming passively. He was, in fact, shouting out the commands to abandon the aircraft so loudly that our dad was awakened and came in to check on him. Dad shook my brother awake to pull him out of his nightmare.

My brother said that possibly the strangest aspect of the dream came afterward. It was weird, he said, but he had complete knowledge of that B-25 aircraft. Upon hearing his story, I understood why he had been reluctant to tell others about it.

I should add that Allen was, and continues to be, fascinated with aviation. As a child, he built and flew model planes. He earned his pilot's license in his teens, and went on to get his instrument, multiengine, and instructor's licenses. During his career as a small business owner, he flew aircraft to meet with clients in other cities. In retirement, he flies World War II-vintage aircraft. Not surprisingly, the vintage planes he has owned have all been models that were used as trainers during the war.

There is another twist to Allen's story. While he was still running his company, a B-25 bomber showed up at the airfield he used. It was the same type as the one in his dream. Allen got involved with the group that had restored the plane – and eventually became its head pilot. When I asked him how it felt to fly the bomber, he answered, "It was like coming home."

While being involved with the B-25, he also was able to get some flight time in a B-17, known as the Flying Fortress. His dream, or nightmare, foreshadowed a lot about his life. Wonders never cease.

That conversation with my brother on the morning of the memorial service was another turning point. I realized that my experiences, and my reluctance to share them, might not be so unique. It was time to take some risks with those around me. The deaths of my father and brother-in-law within weeks of each other also provided some insight on how differently death can be viewed. In my 92-year-old dad's case, since he had been bedridden for a few years, we welcomed his death. He was finally released from a body that no longer served him, and instead had become a source of significant pain. His death was understandable, and we considered it a blessing.

But when it came to my brother-in-law, we were devastated. He was only 61 and had recently been given an excellent report from his cardiologist. Why was it his time to transition? When viewing death as a loss, it felt tragic. It would take some time for me to realize that death is also a rebirth.

Thankfully, there would be a joyous glimmer of hope. It would be the hope of a partner – one with whom I could share all the dimensions of myself, from the professional to the spiritual and everything in between.

Given all that had happened during Years One and Two, I often felt unsure of my direction in life as I journeyed on my new spiritual explorations. There seemed to be countless things to study, meditations to try, mentors with whom to work, and intriguing spiritual dimensions to explore. Does all of this sound familiar?

I was privileged to hear the late author Rob Grant speak during Year Two. He was asked the following questions: "How do we know we are on the right path?" and "How do we know we are working with the right people?" These are difficult questions; yet, Rob provided some intriguing answers by way of his own set of questions.

"Is the path or philosophy grounded in love or fear?" he asked. He suggested that many faiths are built on fear, guilt or unworthiness, instead of love. "My advice is to choose love," he said in a humorous tone.

Rob's next question was, "Does what you are pursuing help you be a better X?" In response to our confused looks, he explained that "X" represented anything important to us; a role to which we aspired. For example, was our current path helping us be a better father, friend or co-worker?

He finished his questions by asking, "Are you working with people who are helping you discover who you are (in other words, to "know thyself"), or are they telling you what to do, who to be, and how to be?" He suggested that great teachers build independence and strength. And great teachers understand that they, too, are evolving. Khalil Gibran's *The Prophet* suggests that great teachers lead us to ourselves. The truth is that both teachers and students are on the road to enlightenment.

Rob pointed out that less enlightened teachers evoke fear or guilt, or act to aggrandize themselves or their organizations. To gauge the motivation of a teacher or organization, Rob suggested looking at the teacher or organization's rules for behavior and thought, and determine if gatekeepers have been placed in the way of a direct connection to Source.

Rob's questions served as guideposts for my Quest, and still do to this day. I hope these questions help guide you in each experience on your own quest:
- Is this grounded in love?
- Is this strengthening my connection to Source?
- Am I coming to know myself better?
- Am I becoming a better X?

YEAR THREE
Starstruck and Stargate

Spring

Revealing the Shadow

By Year Three of my Quest, Amy – who identified the white stallion as my Knight's steed in the earlier Intuition workshop – had become a friend. She brought to my attention the upcoming Omega Institute Conference, to be held in New York City, and urged me to attend. The idea of attending another spiritual event with her was appealing, but part of me resisted. Despite Amy's company and the impressive list of speakers – including Wayne Dyer and Caroline Myss – my reluctance was twofold. First, I had never been comfortable in the Big Apple, with the crowds and the frenetic energy, even though I grew up near it. Moreover, my previous experience of flying to a spiritually-oriented event was still fresh enough to make me wary. Did I want to tempt fate again?

Thanks to Amy's encouragement, I signed up; and when the time came, we flew to New York together. I was grateful that the plane left on time and it was an easy flight. Maybe my luck was changing?

At the Omega conference, the first mini-session I attended was with Debbie Ford, author of many books, including *The Dark Side of the Light Chasers*. Debbie did a great job of explaining why aspects that we dislike of ourselves – and others – are clues about what we need to accept, forgive and integrate. These feelings live in what she called our "shadow side." Our shadow side is the emotional equivalent of a storage area where we stuff all broken or painful things we cannot let go. They are out of sight and often out of mind, but all the things we put in there still exist. We rediscover them when we accidentally "open the door" – or when someone else does.

A focal point of my life has been staying in shape and maintaining an acceptable weight. This has been driven by the "fat kid" in my shadow; I grew up as the heaviest member of both my family and my class at school. By the time I entered high school, I was 5 foot, 6 inches tall, and weighed over 200 pounds – and no, it was not muscle.

I must have needed my world to reflect criticism and judgment at that time, because my physical presence often generated instant derision. I still remember the sting of a comment made by a classmate when I was a sophomore in high school. I walked past him in the gym locker room, and I heard him say to another guy, "If I looked like that, I'd kill myself."

For much of my youth, I transferred that external criticism into internal self-hatred. Later in high school, I vowed that my weight would not be a detriment, and I starved off the excess pounds. It became an obsession to stay on the thin side.

In the Omega workshop, Debbie taught us that we sometimes focus on something because we fear being its opposite – a "shadow side" aspect. In my case, my body image became significant to my long-term identity. I saw no reason to examine the internal pain and anger that drove me to stay thin. Nor did I want to relive the difficult experiences that motivated me to exercise and eat well.

However, I discovered in Debbie's session that avoiding buried pain limits growth and can make it impossible to be at peace. To resolve buried pain, Debbie guided each of us through a meditation to meet one of our shadow selves. These are dimensions of ourselves, often fear-based, that we do not want to see. So, in my meditation, I met Elizabeth.

As I follow Debbie's guidance to relax and meet my shadow, I perceive a hunched figure before me. She tells me her name is Elizabeth, and by all appearances she is homeless. She's wearing a shabby dress and has weathered features. Everything about her suggests that she lives a hard life, and that she is carrying a great burden. Yet, as she approaches me, she smiles and gives me a heart-shaped medal. From somewhere inside me, I understand that this medal symbolizes my heart, which needs to open more fully in order to wield the sword of love. And in the next moment, the Sword materializes between us, pointing skyward. We both take hold of its handle and Elizabeth channels pure energy into the sword.

Then, the entire scene melted away.

The experience was humbling. This woman was dressed in rags, her long hair was disheveled, and she appeared to need my help. The truth, however, was the reverse – she was lending her energy to help me awaken to myself. The message was to **not** shy away from those ugly things in myself. There are gifts in the bedraggled and broken parts within us. What a helpful new way to look at things!

What fears and struggles did I push into my shadow self – like the Knight's battle scene – because they were too painful for me to handle? Childhood and adolescence can leave plenty of painful scars that are difficult to revisit, and easy to avoid. But those scars might be just the tip of the iceberg, if we consider the possibility that we have experienced other lives. My experience with Elizabeth left a lingering question: *What else is in my shadow and how can it be healed?*

That question, and more like it, are part of the Quest that continues to this day.

Another session on the conference schedule that caught my attention was on the topic of intuition. Who would not want more of that? I never considered myself intuitive and I had always been impressed by some of the gifted intuitives I had encountered, including Kimberly and David. Being able to read others – or to receive messages that go beyond what our normal senses perceive – can be quite useful. I decided to attend the session.

What I did not anticipate was that it would be so relevant to my Quest. It was conducted by Lynn Robinson, author of *Intuition Made Easy*. Lynn took us through a guided meditation that brought more hope to my Knight's journey.

I find myself on the same battlefield that I experienced during David's workshop. I am standing once again on the hill, awaiting my death at the hands of the oncoming peasant soldiers.

But this time the battlefield scene is different. I am holding the sword above my head parallel to the ground, and it shines with a blinding intensity. A pure cylinder-shaped shield of brilliant white light envelops me and its power illuminates the entire area. Its light streams out in every direction and up into the heavens. The peasant soldiers cannot penetrate it.

Tears of joy and gratitude flowed down my cheeks. I knew from seeing this brief scene that I no longer needed to fight. Once again, it was about allowing the sword to be an instrument of love. The flashback also signaled to me that many of the battles I had fought – internally and externally – were no longer necessary.

I was evolving from a warrior to a messenger of peace. The next challenge was to figure out how to embody the messenger of peace in my current life. Could I heed the message of peace, or would my old patterns persist and gain more power over me?

What Color Was That Traffic Light?

Not much time had passed after the Omega conference when a strange thing began to happen. I had a recurring problem at traffic lights. While waiting for the red light to turn green, I would begin to react as if the light had changed – even though it had not. This did not just happen a few times, but on an ongoing basis – as if someone or something was prompting me that the light had turned green and it was time to go. This phenomenon would happen most often when I was the first car in line at the light. Fortunately, my car had a manual transmission, and the extra steps involved to engage the clutch and put it in gear saved me several times from pulling out into oncoming traffic.

When the traffic light problem first arose, I thought it was because I was unfocused due to life's transitions coming more rapidly. While I had always been a bit absent-minded, keeping my attention in the everyday world of three-dimensional reality was proving even more challenging. And, of course, it was not acceptable to endanger others on the road. So I concentrated on slowing down my response at lights and double-checking the color of the traffic light before proceeding.

When I mentioned what was happening with the lights to Kimberly, she exclaimed that the same thing was happening to her. In her case, she had actually pulled out into an intersection on a red light. To her amazement, the oncoming car had not hit her – although it was a close call.

Another person working with Kimberly and attending her workshops was not so lucky. He ended up in a serious accident when he pulled out into an intersection on a red light. An oncoming car broadsided him – his car was totaled – and he sustained significant injuries. When I talked to him about the accident, he said he was sure that the light had turned green. But a witness at the scene reported that the light had not changed, so he was at fault.

Why were we experiencing this phenomenon? I could understand if it was just me zoning out, which goes with being a professor. But how could three of us, separated by thousands of miles in Georgia, Texas and Oregon, experience the same challenge and – for one of us, at least – have it lead to serious injury? There was something there that seemed to be bending the normal rules of reality.

Since the appearance of the Knight, my world had shifted in unexpected ways. Each step was another venture into the unknown, and often those steps were accompanied by fear. On many a day, I asked myself: *What have I gotten myself into? What does all of this mean?*

Kimberly and I spent considerable time talking about what might have been happening, and why. Were we being warned of dangers awaiting us if we continued? Should we not proceed any further with our spiritual explorations? While those questions could possibly apply to what had happened to our friend, we both felt that it was our own fears trying to dissuade us. We needed to look deeper.

The best explanation we could come up with was that the traffic light issue was orchestrated by our egos. The ego wants us to think we are our bodies, and only our bodies, and that the physical realm is our only reality – in essence, that we are mere mortals. We, on the other hand, were endeavoring to transcend our egos and three-dimensional reality. Maybe the best way to pull us back, to "get our heads out of the clouds," as my father used to say, was through an accident.

Connecting with Source and knowing that we are not bound by what we are experiencing on the physical level is a threat to the ego. According to some, the ego will do anything to thwart expansive spiritual journeys (Renard, 2004). What better way to force us to attend to the here and now than to mire us in car, health, and insurance problems?

What amazed me was how subtle the attempts were to divert our focus. The efforts to keep us from moving forward did not come in overt ways; people did not challenge our beliefs or confront us physically. Of course, in past times, people who disagreed with accepted religious practices were tortured and killed.

Whatever the ultimate reason was for what we experienced at the stoplights, it did not feel as if the Knight within me had previously dealt with these more subtle challenges. I needed to become more aware – even in such mundane situations as waiting for traffic lights to change. Buddhists call this way of thinking "being mindful." My Knight had to learn to function in the modern world although he was more used to a world of chivalry where his enemy was on the battlefield, and his stallion always knew the way home.

One clear message was: no matter what I was discovering spiritually, I also needed to be fully aware of the here and now. I chose to have the Knight's life and it was important to my journey. Until my Knight decided to let his life end, he needed to be focused and ready to use his skills to survive. In my current life, I too needed to stay focused, although in more subtle ways. That meant I needed to be ready for high-speed traffic in and around Atlanta – losing myself in a spiritual reverie was not an option.

Riding the Stallion

Although the white stallion had appeared to me five months earlier, in the fall, I had not attempted to connect with him in any meaningful way. However, like most things on my journey, a shift in that relationship came unexpectedly.

David was conducting another workshop for our group. In one exercise, we each stood in front of the group while he shined a variety of colored lights on us – one color at a time. He explained that different aspects of us would be revealed through the different light frequencies. The rest of the group would report what they could "see" under the various colors.

When it was my turn to be in front, I was not expecting much to happen. I envisioned holding the Shield on my left side to possibly give the others something to perceive. I intentionally did not imagine the Sword, because I was afraid that its appearance might have unintended consequences.

After closing my eyes, I feel myself holding the Shield with my left arm. I realize I am astride a huge horse; it is the white stallion. He is mammoth. His back is so wide that I wonder how I am able to get my legs around his massive expanse.

His head is clad in gleaming battle armor. Enemy soldiers are arrayed across the opposite hills; a gentle undulating plain stretches out before us. The enemy is at such a distance that I cannot make out their uniforms or weapons; I only know that they span the entire horizon. My stallion stands motionless, with no sign of nervousness. This is our job, and we are awaiting the order to engage.

I hear David's voice as if from afar, and he asks me why my right wrist is glowing. I tell him I am holding the reins of my stallion with that hand. He remarks that it makes sense. Feelings of happiness arise in me, and I open my eyes.

While mounted on the stallion was a shift in my past-life experiences, I believe that the most important messages were the subtle ones. When we stood facing the enemy and awaiting the battle, there was no panic or fear. Together, we would function as one, and we would do what needed to be done. There was a merging of purpose that would empower us to be effective.

So, what did I need to merge with to feel that same calm and purpose in my current life? The answer led once again to Source.

Raphael and the Crown

As I continued on my Ultimate Quest, I often wondered if my spiritual experiences were just for me to keep to myself, or if I was meant to share them in some way. This book answers that question, but at the time I was not sure.

I continued to sense the presence of a visitor during my daily meditations. There was a being of light with me, but my perception of him or her was so indistinct that I initially did not pay much attention to it. I even thought that it could have been my imagination, because images would often come and go during my meditations.

One evening, the being's presence felt stronger, so I asked for a name. I understood the response to be "Raphael." A few days later, as I settled into my evening meditation, Raphael appeared to me, and that was when my meditations became more interesting.

Raphael is standing before me holding a crown. It is bejeweled and made of gold – it reminds me of the sword. Is it a symbol? A guidepost? A gift? The vision fades from view.

That was it for that meditation, but a few days later, Raphael reappeared.

Raphael is standing before me and puts the crown on my head. Feelings of unworthiness flow over me. What does this mean? This crown is befitting a king, but not me. The crown and Raphael fade away.

A few weeks later, I had a reading with an intuitive friend, and I asked her if she could help me understand Raphael's appearances. She tuned in to the situation, and soon suggested that Raphael's presence was not a short-term visitation. Raphael was in my life to lend guidance and to assure me of my worthiness.

Our first collaboration was to write this book.

While I had many research publications to my credit, offering spiritual guidance to others was new territory. I will admit, the potential to touch hearts and enrich the lives of others was exciting, humbling and overwhelming. However, I had plenty of self-doubt. How could I tell a story where the plot was fuzzy, the narrative was still unfolding with no ending, and there were many interpretations – with one explanation: I was crazy? Could I write about what was happening in my life in a way that would make sense to others?

As I pondered these questions in the days following my reading, I could not see how sharing my confusion and struggles would do anything but discourage others. The field of spiritual teachers already had plenty of people – like Wayne Dyer and Dan Millman – to point the way. While I was well-versed in my professional field, and could speak with some authority there, this Quest was a completely different world. I was still trying to find my way. But, in the years that followed, my guides made it clear that I did have a message to share.

A few weeks after I received the clarification about Raphael, I received an email from a friend who had taken part in two of Kimberly's workshops. In her email, she said she had information for me. She told me I now had two archangels working with me – Raphael and Raziel. When I saw her reference to Raphael, I broke out laughing. What an incredible and unexpected confirmation! I felt more confident now that I knew that Archangel Raphael and Archangel Raziel were guiding me, and that the crown was about me sharing my journey. How it all was going to unfold – and when – would be revealed in time. At least, I sure hoped so.

Summer

A Surprise Guest

The more we explore who we are, the more we may desire someone with whom to share the journey. I wanted to believe that someday, a partner – like the one foreshadowed in my former journey up the mountain where I received the Shield and Sword – would come into my life.

It was time for Kimberly's third workshop, which would be held at my home since she was still staying with me. And since the workshop would be at my place, my faithful companion (Sir) Fulton could be involved – he loved participating. Even though the previous two workshops had been transforming, I could not have fathomed what was coming.

The surprises began the moment the others arrived at my door. When Fulton and I returned from our morning walk and approached the house, several cars were already in the driveway. With a few pangs of guilt – mine, not

Fulton's – because we were not there to greet our guests, we walked in the front door.

I was planning to say a quick hello to the others and make a hasty exit to the shower. I certainly was not expecting one of the new participants, Jen, to rock my world. When our eyes met, I was lost in the depths of her bluish-green gaze. After I regained some of my composure, I took in the rest of her. She was adorable, on the slender side, with shoulder-length light brown hair, and her smile lit me up. I suddenly felt self-conscious, standing there in my shorts and sweaty T-shirt.

While making my departure as gracefully as possible, I caught a glimpse of Kimberly. She gave me a knowing smile that spoke volumes, but provided no details. The weekend had suddenly taken a most unexpected turn.

With Fulton at my heels, I bounded up the stairs to my bedroom. Closing the door behind us, I looked at Fulton. He locked in on me, as if asking, "What just happened?" I did not have an answer; and I knew it would not make any sense to him even if I had one.

I jumped in the shower. Nervous as a cat on a hot tin roof, I needed to get a hold of myself quickly. While dressing, I tried to calm down by focusing on my breathing. *Everything is going to be OK,* I told myself.

The workshop began smoothly. I settled down and focused on what I needed to do. Kimberly announced that in our first exercise, we would explore our deepest fears with a selected partner – her choice, not ours. Working with our fears was a theme throughout the weekend. We were urged – to the greatest extent possible – to be open and introspective.

To my shock, Kimberly paired me with Jen. I suspected that Kimberly did it on purpose, given my initial reaction. I knew that Kimberly had a mean streak!

Great. Now I was to reveal my deepest, darkest fears to a woman I had just met. And, I was attracted to her. To add insult to injury, I was to go first. My most immediate concern was to not look like a damn fool in front of this woman. *What could I say that would be honest – and, at the same time, would not cast me in a negative light?*

I decided to talk about my fear of failure, and of being a target of criticism and rejection. Most times when I got attention, especially during my youth, it was as the fat kid with a reading disability. It was not good. And although I shed the weight over the years, and learned ways around my reading problem, my subconscious had not received those messages. I still spent a lot of energy being on alert for negative attention.

Since I had just met Jen, I was not willing to share my history of embarrassment with her. Old fears came to the surface – this cute female was sitting across from me, and I was not going there, at least not with many details.

I provided what I thought was a reasonable "executive summary." Trying to make a good impression – while baring my soul – was not easy. Have you ever had the feeling of walking a tightrope without a safety net? That summed up my dilemma.

Jen's job was to listen and then comment on my revelations. It was soon evident, however, that she did not find my depth of self-understanding impressive. Given the situation, I admit that I skirted some of my significant fears.

We moved through my part of the exercise, and then it was her turn. The fear she shared was that of never finding a partner for her life's journey of spirit and love. I wanted to ask her to take a look at the guy sitting across from her as a possible candidate, but I knew how absurd that would sound – we had just met! I tried hard to dismiss my response to her as simply a normal male reaction, and did my best to keep an even composure. My focus was on my self-development throughout the weekend – at least, that was where I tried to keep it.

Later that same day, as the group was breaking for lunch, Kimberly signaled to Sara and me that we had extra work to do. She asked us to revisit the lifetime we had together as knights. I thought that Kimberly would provide some additional explanation, but she did not. So, along with the rest of the group, she headed toward the kitchen.

As the group departed, Sara and I were kidded by the others about having to do extra work. We joked that we were special and therefore deserved additional time. Those departing for lunch bought none of it.

Once the room cleared, we positioned our chairs opposite each other so that our knees were almost touching. We reviewed what Kimberly had said about our task to revisit the time where we were knights together. We settled ourselves, closed our eyes, and separately asked to be taken to what we most needed to see from that lifetime together.

I am a knight and envision Sara as a page supporting me. Then, the image fades. She is now a knight standing before me, but something is different. There is no joy coming from her. My god, she never wanted to be a knight! She flourished being my support person and staying out of the brutal fray. I pushed her into knighthood, and I was the one who wanted her recognized. She never wanted to join in the bloodshed.

She entered the slaughter to protect me because of love. Guilt arises like bile in my throat. The horror I brought her into was what I wanted, and what I believed to be a great honor. How could I push her into knighthood and then later abandon it myself? How could I ever forgive myself? My tears flow.

I told Sara all of what I felt – and with tears of regret, I did my best to apologize. There was a flash of recognition from her as she too realized that she had never wanted to fight. With reluctance, she verified my vision, but her facial reaction suggested there was far more to her experience than she wanted to reveal. She did not tell me what she witnessed, nor did I press her for the details.

We talked a few days after the workshop, and she maintained that it was a past lifetime and no longer relevant. There was no willingness on her part to pursue the matter – period. I sensed that whatever was behind the door we opened was too painful for her to explore.

I have seen the same thing happen with myself and others. We create safeguards to protect us from areas that would be too overwhelming to examine or re-experience. In some cases, people who have been severely traumatized can block all memory of an event. At least some inner part of Sara was flashing her a warning sign, and it was safer to tell herself that it no longer mattered.

Sara never returned to the workshops after that, and soon withdrew from my life. I felt that I had failed to make things right, and I took responsibility for what happened to our relationship. Only later did I accept – reluctantly – that love means respecting others' choices. It was a huge lesson for me and the Knight within, who had believed that his job was to rescue everyone he loved.

Throughout the rest of the workshop, I did my utmost to keep my attraction to Jen to myself. Yet, everything that happened between us, and seeing how she interacted with the others, only heightened my interest. She was bright and witty, with a serious side when it came to her career and her spirituality. And, during one of our conversations, I learned that she was 11 years younger than I was. I recognized that might be significant.

My attempts at keeping my attraction to her secret turned out to be futile. It was difficult, if not impossible, to hide such things from a group that was working on intuitive abilities. It was, in fact, a source of great amusement. Almost everyone picked up on my reaction to Jen, and a few had spoken privately to each other about what might be happening.

As our weekend was ending, I decided I needed to be honest with Jen – assuming she too had picked up on at least some of my feelings. I steeled myself for the likely outcome that she was not interested.

While the rest of the group was relaxing, I asked Jen if we could talk. Once we found some privacy, I shared my feelings. I told her that my attraction did not mean that I expected her to reciprocate. I said that I knew she was younger than I was, and that there were plenty of reasons for her to say, "No, thank you." My thoughts were bouncing between a desperate hope of her having some interest in me, and the greater chance of me making a complete fool of myself. I have been known to do that on occasion.

I finished my piece and waited for a response. She looked at me and smiled warmly. Somewhere in her response, she admitted feeling a passion between us. I could not remember her exact words; my thoughts were all over the place. Was it possible that the hoped-for partner had walked into my life two days earlier?

In no uncertain terms, I was falling for her.

After chatting for a few more minutes, we rejoined the group. I then asked her son, who was also at the workshop, if we could have a brief chat. I thought it might be a nice gesture to ask for his OK to date his mother. Upon hearing my question, he jumped up and shouted, "I knew it; I just knew it!"

"Does this mean yes?"

"Of course it does!"

We hugged and then rejoined the group. Not surprisingly, there was a chair left open for me beside Jen. I sat there glowing while trying to take part in the discussion about the weekend's experiences. I admit that I found the conversation much less interesting than the thoughts swimming in my head – visions of building a life with the woman sitting beside me.

Jen and I faced formidable barriers. She lived over 2,000 miles away, had two children, and worked ridiculous hours. Once she arrived back at her home, we had a long talk on the phone that included ideas on how we could spend time together. I wanted to fly out to her place as soon as possible, but she wanted to come back to visit me so we could spend time together without the influence of her family. I agreed, and looked forward to seeing her in six weeks' time.

Knights can be misunderstood in matters of love. They are – at least in mythology – rescuers of damsels in distress. What knight can resist drawing his sword to protect and defend a woman in need? But rescuing a maiden and building a lifetime partnership are different. The Knight in me knew that his true love would possess her own strength, and would be an equal on the journey of discovery.

Jen felt like such a match for me. She was not in distress – she exuded strength, and had the playful quality of the partner who had escorted me up the mountain in my earlier vision. The Knight in me was ready to mount his stallion and ride by her side.

I later came to understand that my reaction to Jen went beyond her beauty and energy. It was a soul-level recognition. There are people who hit us at a deep level. We have already known them on a level that transcends their current characteristics, such as how they look or what activities in which they are involved. That type of recognition can lead to strong feelings, either positive or negative, based on experiences with them from other lifetimes. From what I could tell, my path and Jen's had crossed in other times and places. Based on my reactions to her, I guessed that we had shared positive experiences.

Eagerly, I looked forward to discovering more about her, and discovering more with her.

Once a Vow, Always a Vow

As the recent experiences of my Quest had shown me, remembering our past lives can help us to better understand our gifts and the challenges in our current life. For example, do you have an aversion to something – an aversion that makes no logical sense? It could be part of a remembrance from a past-life experience. As my Knight was showing me, there is much to discover about ourselves in our past.

While working with Kimberly, I was trying to change my feelings of being a victim, and change my mindset so I could understand how to hold onto happiness and joy. She was using theta-level healing, which operates on the energy frequency that allows us to access the subconscious (see footnote 1). The essence of the technique is to connect with Source – the origin of pure love – and to use that Source energy for healing.

No matter what we did, things did not shift for me. I continued to feel the need to look over my proverbial shoulder, waiting for the next shoe to drop. Kimberly said that we might be challenging some vows I had made in past lives – decisions deeply embedded in my subconscious. She explained that in past lifetimes, people often took vows of poverty or chastity, or renounced joy and pleasure, believing that these commitments were necessary to receive God's grace. Most people living on earth now, she said, have probably had lifetimes in monastic settings – where self-denial and sacrifice were mainstays of spirituality. And, while it might seem logical that we would make a fresh start in each new lifetime, such vows do not seem to expire.

My Knight believed that sacrificing his life would bring an end to the moral battle raging inside of him. He would be disappointed to discover that the vows he took had no expiration date, but rather continued through subsequent lifetimes. His sacrifice in that lifetime only delayed him (me) from facing a fundamental truth. He believed that taking those vows would bring him closer to Christ, which was his Quest in that era. Instead, those vows actually kept him away from what he most desired – a Christ-consciousness and the understanding of love.

Although human spirituality has evolved since the days of the knights, old vows can continue to exert a significant influence in our lives. A friend of mine had made a vow of poverty in a past life. She admitted that the more successful she became, the more conflicted and guilty she felt. Past-life vows may help explain why we continue to create undesired outcomes, even after years of self-exploration and counseling. Are we sabotaging ourselves because we are trying to uphold former vows? My experience says, **yes.**

Using a form of applied kinesiology, or muscle testing (see footnote 2), I discovered that I had sworn to an entire array of vows, especially those having to do with eschewing joy and pleasure. Despite my efforts to remove those vows with the theta-level technique, they stayed intact.

I needed to figure out why I was still holding onto them. Beliefs and vows are arrayed in a hierarchy within us. Trying to shift the ones at the surface will often be unsuccessful if the ones further below are left in place.

My Knight had vowed to uphold his covenants to the medieval Roman Catholic Church, which meant renouncing everything that might interfere with the church's accepted view of purity. In medieval times, the view of purity was harsh and austere. In one meditation, when I was attempting to release the vows, I experienced being branded with the side of a red-hot sword – to burn those vows into my soul. Thankfully, none of my current flesh was harmed – but no wonder the vows were proving so difficult to release.

A consequence of taking such extreme vows is that we come to believe that we need to be perfect to be worthy in God's eyes. I sure did. I had spent much of this lifetime trying to be above reproach. That standard fits with the knight in shining armor, doesn't it? The belief that I must be perfect manifested itself in feelings of never being satisfied with what I accomplished, and never feeling good enough. Instead, I focused on my shortcomings. Because shortcomings were always easy to find, self-criticism became entrenched in my internal dialogue. My entire world felt judgmental, but that reflected what was inside me. So, I worked tirelessly to avoid others' criticism and tried to maintain a sterling image.

I came to realize that perfection, as I perceived it, is unattainable. It is like a dog chasing its own tail – no matter how hard he tries to catch it, the tail is still out of reach.

I saw plenty of signs in my life of the vows I was still holding. If something evoked a negative emotional response, it signaled that I was hanging on to limiting or detrimental beliefs.

Those kinds of signs were part of my experience with my first serious girlfriend. Her family's standard of love included a strong sense of sacrifice. For example, her parents emphasized what they were giving up for their children. In her family, the way to prove love was by making sacrifices for those other family members.

I was aware that if I wanted to be in her life, I would need to abandon my "unrealistic ideas" of a more rewarding career and remain in my stable, corporate position. For her part, she told me how much she appreciated that I was working in a job I did not like. That demonstrated to her that I understood what it would take to build a life and family together.

During the time we dated, I recoiled from her sacrificial model of love. Yet, later I realized how much it was ingrained in me. What I saw in her and her family was in me as well. My Knight was steeped in that same notion of sacrificing for what he loved. Although ultimately I decided it would be best to separate from her, I felt guilty about hurting her. She believed that she loved me and wanted us to spend the rest of our lives together. Holding on to my guilt probably reinforced my vow of sacrifice, even though I had no clue it was in me at the time.

I also discovered how vows can continue to play a role in our daily lives. The vows within me to eschew things like joy made it easy for me to judge others. I would see them as not taking their lives or careers seriously enough. Even when I was off playing, it felt like I was stealing time from other more worthwhile endeavors. To compensate for my underlying feelings, my play became work-like. The purpose of riding with the cycling club was to help me become faster and to build endurance. Time at home was not focused on leisure, but on projects to improve the value of my house. When I was not striving toward some goal, I would often feel anxious. I did not want to waste precious time.

My spirituality has shifted a lot from the medieval times in which I took the original vows. Gratitude and joy are now the keys to my spiritual practice; but back in those earlier incarnations, I believed God's grace was earned through pain and sacrifice. I thought that God was punitive. While those vows may have served my Knight, they were no longer serving me. The vows needed to be released.

I also came to realize that feelings of guilt carry a strong energy and can even recall or reactivate vows we believe we have released. Moreover, when we do release vows, their removal can leave gaps in our identity. If we hold vows of sacrifice and suffering, their removal can affect how we relate to ourselves.

I saw this happen with a friend. We were working on examining and removing her vows of poverty and austerity. Soon, I could sense her panic – not only in her words, but also in the pit of my stomach. We then worked to build her a new identity that allowed for joy and abundance. For a few days, she struggled with withdrawal from her previous, familiar beliefs. She felt lost during the transition; but she soon discovered more of who she was without such vows. It turned out that I was going to be challenged by my own vows for a while as well.

Falling Hard

Do you remember what it is like to fall in love? You think you have found the person of your dreams – the one with whom you want to build a life. Life feels lighter, challenges are less formidable, and the possibilities of what you can accomplish together are unlimited. The more time you spend together, the better it feels.

After we met and connected at the workshop, Jen and I talked on the phone almost every day. I learned about her life as a single mom with two children. Her son, I knew; her daughter, I looked forward to meeting. She also shared her many work-related trials and triumphs with me. She was in the grocery industry, and her job was to set up and launch new stores. I admired her dedication to her job and the people with whom she worked – and how consistently she pulled off the task of getting stores ready to open on time. I could only imagine the pressure she was under with each new store opening.

When she returned to visit, we had a wonderful time. It was just us, and everything in our interactions told me I had found a partner – maybe even The Partner. I will never forget the sight of her trim, athletic body moving up the trail ahead of me as we hiked up a local mountain. The physical attraction was almost overwhelming, and my thoughts often wandered far beyond the status of our relationship at that point. I was falling hard for her, and I was making plans on how to put our lives together.

At the top of the mountain, we sat and watched an entire flock of turkey vultures "riding the thermals" – soaring in the air currents created by the wind flowing up the side of the mountain. It was remarkable how majestic such ungainly – some might say ugly – birds could be in flight.

Jen told me that she had seen hundreds of birds of prey during a recent drive to see her family in California. She explained that they symbolize lifelong partnerships, because they mate for life. I took this as another confirmation that my true partner was by my side. We leaned into each other, with her hand in mine. My entire being was illuminated with a yearning for us to be together. Whatever it was going to take, I was all-in.

Being with Jen made life so much better. We enjoyed sitting and watching movies together. Even something mundane, like going to the grocery store, was a more joyous experience when she was with me. It was an education to see the aisles and shelves through her eyes.

We were well-matched and walking similar spiritual paths. It was wonderful to sit and talk about the spiritual journeys we were traveling. There was a genuine desire on both of our parts to move forward, and also to help those around us. There was not one thing she shared with me that raised a red flag. One evening, to my delight, I discovered another mutual interest.

While driving to dinner – on our second evening together – a classic car passed us on the highway. I noticed Jen looking at it with genuine interest, so I asked her, "If you could have any classic car, what would you choose?"

"Oh, a Shelby GT 350 of course."

Surprised by her definite, no-hesitation response, I had to ask, "Why not the GT 500, the more powerful version?"

"Because the 350 is far better balanced."

I suspect that my quizzical look caused her to pick up on my astonishment at her knowledge. And yes, I realized I was being sexist. Before I could inquire further, she continued, "I assisted in my high school's auto shop for two years and have always been interested in cars."

When we arrived at the restaurant and got out of the car, she slipped her hand in mine as we walked toward the door. That simple act spoke volumes. Our connectedness flooded me with an indescribable joy – and, I swear, I was at least a foot taller. It felt like she was committed to exploring a life with me. Rarely had I ever been so sure about something. I wanted a life with Jen.

It was as if Jen had stepped out of my dream. She was all I longed for, and more than I could have imagined. I felt sure that we could handle the myriad number of challenges we faced; the major one would be to figure out where we would live together. Until then, we would be frequent fliers.

I was going to Florida for a professional conference at the end of October, and there was another workshop scheduled at my home in Atlanta in early November. We decided to rendezvous in Florida and then fly together to the workshop. Considering the cost of hotel rooms, we opted to share one. Did that mean things were progressing to the next level – a more intimate connection? I hoped so with all of my being.

It was summer, and I would not be with Jen until fall. While I would miss her, there would be plenty of teaching and research for me to do in my profession – and also a lot of spiritual growth on which to work – even more than I realized.

Preparing for the Unknown

I believed that everything I was doing was divinely guided, but I was about to learn some difficult lessons. No one ever said that spiritual growth is easy. In fact, growth usually happens outside of our comfort zone – and I was about to be really uncomfortable.

Believe it or not, our bodies can react in unpleasant ways when we make positive changes in our health habits. For example, people report terrible withdrawal symptoms when they give up smoking, making it hard to quit. In my experience, spiritual breakthroughs can create similar reactions. As we adjust to new energies, and our minds shift to new understandings, old beliefs and core values resist being resolved or replaced. It can be downright painful.

I do not remember how the idea emerged, but the group that had formed from the workshops led by David, Shawn and Kimberly received a message that we had something special to do at an upcoming mountaintop retreat. Kimberly told us all to ask our guides for more information. She also warned us that the weeks ahead might be challenging.

Meanwhile, I was working to remove the remaining vows that were holding me back. I was using the same theta-level healing technique as before, but I became sick as a dog. My fears and buried commitments were putting up a valiant fight – darn them!

Also during that time, Kimberly was struggling to handle what she understood to be higher frequencies of light and love. I watched her experience pain, discomfort and sleeplessness. She knew she would have a key role to play at the retreat; but none of us realized what the full significance of her role would be.

I do not remember the precise details of how we figured out our mission at the retreat. It just seemed to emerge as we considered possibilities. We determined that we were meant to open a stargate. This was unknown territory for me. I actually did not have a clue what a stargate was – other than something in a science-fiction novel. Were they energy portals that spaceships fly through, in order to jump to other parts of the universe at hyper-speed?

I turned to the internet for information. Some of the explanations were highly technical. From what little I understood, these stargate openings allow vast amounts of energy to flow between different realities, such as universes or dimensions.

I knew that our group wanted to bring more healing energy to Mother Earth. So, as a neophyte, I focused my efforts on preparation. The details of opening a stargate far surpassed my level of scientific knowledge, and I hoped that those particulars would not be important to what I was called to do.

Over the next few weeks, we worked to transform our anger, resentment and fear into love and gratitude, so we could channel more clearly (see footnote 1). None of us had it as difficult as Kimberly, whose job was to receive all of the energy to open the stargate. Then, the group would be able to project that energy out into the world.

Kimberly tried to connect more fully to Source's love through prayer and by going to the theta level of consciousness, so she could channel the highest amount of energy possible. One evening, she emerged from my guest bedroom looking defeated. With pain-filled eyes, she said, "I am not sure I can do this! This is killing me!" I offered to help her figure out what was happening.

I close my eyes, tune into her suffering, and get a real shock. I see a lance coming through her back. The point is lodged in her heart and it has an energetic poison on the tip. *I can only imagine the pain she is experiencing, and I shudder in empathy. No wonder she looks like she is at death's door.*

After telling her what I saw, she closed her eyes and was quiet for a few moments. When she opened her eyes, they were wide with amazement. She said that she had not considered the possibility of something attempting to thwart her efforts by attacking her heart. She closed her eyes again, and then reported success in removing the spear and healing the wound. It was evident that the poison's effects dissipated over the next few days.

The lingering question was: What the hell was attempting to prevent us from opening the stargate? Was I frightened? Yes – this Knight had found himself in an unfamiliar realm where battles were occurring on an energetic level. Therefore, a new kind of armor was needed. *Make mine a size medium – extra thick, please!*

In retrospect, one of the greatest challenges was the uncertainty. What would await us on the mountaintop? Could we even open a stargate; and would we be OK afterward?

As the time for the retreat approached, we pushed hard to be ready. One thing that we found useful was to meditate on the following phrases: *I am of the light, I am the light,* and *I am a source of the light.* I repeated these phrases in my daily meditation, but substituted the word "love" for "the light." The meditations helped put me into the right frame of mind, while infusing myself with the light and protection of love. Calling in the vibration of something that we want helps our minds and bodies transition to a new state of being. It is like gradually warming up a basin of water by repeatedly adding small amounts of hot water.

Throughout all of our preparations, I kept Jen informed about our group's activities and challenges. In particular, I shared our fears that there might be forces opposed to our mission. She was supportive and eager to hear how the stargate opening would unfold. I kept thinking how much I wanted Jen to be at the retreat with me; but I understood that with her work schedule and family, it was not possible. I looked forward to later in the fall, when we would be together again.

Fall

The Stargate Opening

In the fall, our group gathered at an annual retreat; I had been a longtime regular attendee. This was the same retreat where I had the shamanic journey experiences and saw myself in biblical times as a follower of Jesus. My plan was to participate in the official, organized activities, as well as to work with our group to open the stargate. I figured that I could satisfy both responsibilities and keep everyone happy. Once again, I was wonderfully naïve!

Because the group members lived in different parts of the country, we had coordinated our efforts via long-distance phone conversations. Now, we were finally together at the retreat and would need to prepare for the big event. There were seven of us, with Kimberly leading the way.

In our practice sessions, she placed us in a circle, with our backs to her in the center. She brought in as much of Source's energy as she could and then distributed that energy to each of us. No words were spoken – to an observer, we would simply appear to be a group sitting in a circular meditation. I imagine it was a curious sight, though, considering that we were all facing away from each other.

Our job was to project the Source energy from our hearts out toward the horizon. At first, the energy was at a low level; but with each 30-minute practice session, I could feel the energy intensify. I experienced it as a buzzing in my body and as a beam of light being sent out into the world. The only personal manifestation of what we were doing was increasing fatigue – as if something was draining some of our own energy. The more we practiced, the more lethargic we felt. Napping became a key part of our routine.

In between practice sessions and naps, Kimberly did her best to coach each of us on how to be better channels of energy. However, I was afraid of opening my entire being to an invisible energy realm that I could only sense. The Knight within me was struggling with what he could neither see nor touch. The things he had done in the name of faith while on earth had not worked out well – so, releasing that fear became my focus.

Following dinner on the first night of the retreat, Barbara, one of our group members, settled herself on the couch in our living area, looked at me and said, "You have a job to do."

"Do you happen to know what that job is?" I asked, desperately looking for guidance.

"Nope," she said with a bit of smugness. "It is for you to figure out." Her tone made it clear that further questions would be futile.

Feeling deflated, my dinner turned into a lump in my stomach, and I could feel myself starting to sweat. The entire group turned toward me with a collective look of expectation. I glanced over at Kimberly, hoping she would give me a clue. Any hint would be a starting point. All she offered was a shrug, and her expression told me that she, too, was baffled. Questions raced through my mind.

What am I meant to do? This is not my idea, but I am stuck figuring it out. I close my eyes. I ask Source to guide me: If I am to do something for our mission at this retreat, show me the way. Desperately, I plead, "Help me, please!" Focusing on my breath, I try to slow my rapidly-beating heart and stay still enough to receive help.

I envision holding the Sword above me, pointed skyward, and I am inside a narrow vortex with a moderate wind encircling me. I sense that I am to use the Sword to speed up this swirling energy. The energy builds momentum and strength. The vortex feels like a miniature hurricane with me at its center. There is a power surrounding me that surpasses everything but the Sword itself. The vortex becomes self-sustaining, and I return to normal consciousness.

What was my job? I gathered it was to get the energy moving for the stargate opening, and it was another opportunity for me to work with the Sword of love. The impression I had during the experience was that someday, I would handle even higher levels of power, and the Sword would take on even greater significance in my life.

I opened my eyes to everyone watching me. I just said, "It was incredible." I asked the others if they picked up on what had taken place. A few, including Kimberly, gave me knowing smiles. Believing that my job was completed, I gave thanks and experienced a sense of relief.

The following day, we were to open the stargate at 11 p.m. The time was information that Kimberly received during a meditation. I was not surprised that we would be waiting until late in the evening, so we could do the opening after the retreat participants would have settled in for the night.

We gathered after dinner and waited for the appointed hour. While waiting, there was a strange, somber mood that settled over us. The atmosphere felt familiar – except that in the distant past, it would have been the calm before a battle. With the preparations made, the equipment ready, and our strategy set, we would await the call to take up arms.

Now we were taking the field in a different way – no razor-sharp swords, no gleaming shields, no war machines, and no warhorses. We were going in love. This had taken us many lifetimes to learn. Force was not the way; blood was not the way. Yet, the time we spent waiting evoked the same nervous energy in us as before a battle. I had not forgotten what happened to Kimberly's heart – as a result, apprehension nagged at me. What was waiting for us?

At a quarter to 11, we drove up to the main part of the retreat center. Our site for opening the stargate would be a sloping grassy knoll near the center of the retreat's property, with a few scattered trees about the perimeter. The dark sky held a blanket of stars as we arrived and started to prepare.

At that hour everything was quiet, as if the retreat center was holding its breath. There was nothing to indicate that this time or place was anything special. No monument would be dedicated to our efforts, and no one would laud our bravery.

Kimberly stood in the middle of the knoll and then spent a few minutes positioning each of us. My place in the circle was on a modest incline with my back to her and the rest of the group.

I am working to keep my balance as a pulsing energy sent from Kimberly flows through my entire body. I focus on creating a beam of power, emanating from my heart, to send Source energy to the entire world. Time freezes while I flow this love, which I perceive as a pure white beam. From somewhere in the back of my consciousness, I hear Kimberly calling us back from our task.

The actual time that passed was about 40 minutes, but to me it seemed like only a few minutes. We sat on the grass for the better part of an hour and compared notes. Everyone described how some form of energy had flowed from them, and we were elated that we accomplished what we came to do. There was genuine satisfaction in completing our mission.

Kimberly informed us that the full stargate opening would unfold over the next few weeks. Each of us had felt the power. We now felt wedded to this place – we were tired, but aglow, because of what we had accomplished.

In later conversations with Kimberly, she suggested that stargates are openings that allow Mother Earth to draw upon Source's love to raise the frequency of the planet. Opening a stargate would not only make it possible for Mother Earth to shift, but also would provide a more supportive frequency for humankind's ascension.

The Personal Impact

I was proud of what we did in opening the stargate. It was an honor to do it and to, hopefully, bring more love to the world. But, no matter how much it may feel right for us to do something, not everyone will understand it or support it. I was about to learn another difficult lesson. As a friend says, "Even if you save the world, do not expect anyone to applaud."

The efforts we expended to prepare for the stargate opening had left us exhausted. That meant that we had used some of our own energy along with channeling Source. Naps and discussions took priority over attending the program in which we had enrolled. While we managed to go to a few of the formal sessions, we missed a majority of them. The unwritten – but well understood – expectation was that we should have attended those sessions, and we did not. We were conspicuous by our absences. That was especially true for me, since I was a regular at the retreat.

A good friend from California had flown in to attend the retreat with me and be my roommate. Like many others, he was baffled by the activities of our group. I did my best to explain the situation, but to no avail. He said he could not understand what we were doing or why we were doing it. He added that there was uneasiness within the larger retreat group about what we were doing. From what they could see, we were rejecting them and spending time as a clique unto ourselves. Each time my friend left to go to the official sessions without me, I sensed his growing disappointment in me.

On the third night, he moved out of our quarters to find a saner roommate. I felt torn. I believed our small group had a job to do, and had strong feelings of loyalty to them. Yet, my roommate was a close friend who felt hurt and confused by my choices. In his eyes, I had let him down. After the workshop, we would spend time together on the drive to the airport, hopefully repairing our relationship.

Again, my withdrawal into the smaller group raised plenty of eyebrows. And a few of the retreat's other participants who had known me for years let me know of their displeasure. The most blunt assessment came from another good friend; she approached me on the retreat's last morning as I was getting ready to leave.

"Do you know how inappropriate your behavior was this weekend, and how many people are angry with you?"

"I know how it looks, and yes, I have a sense of how many people are angry with me. All I can say is that we had something very important to do. We had a stargate to open. What I did not anticipate was how much it would take me away from the planned program. For that I am sorry."

"That is no excuse! There was a waiting list for this retreat, and you abused the privilege of attending. If you ever come back, you will attend everything. Do I make myself clear?"

"Yes, you do."

She turned and walked away.

That was a punch to the gut, pure and simple. I had stepped outside the norms of this progressive group and had disappointed my friends. I understood why they perceived our group's actions as inappropriate. We had signed up for program slots and did not participate. Yet, we had accomplished what we believed was an amazing feat. I so wanted my friends and others to share our excitement. What was I thinking?

What I received was another lesson about unconditional love. I came up against my judgmental side; I played the victim, the misunderstood, and the unappreciated. As time passed, understanding came. Did those who criticized me deserve my love? Yes. Did it serve me to feel victimized? No. Did I have more to learn? Of course. Sainthood was – and still is – nowhere in sight!

The retreat experience was a "coming out" of sorts. I knew my path ahead would require me to draw the Sword only in love. The Knight's belief that he was duty-bound to draw blood in the name of honor, Christ, or God no longer served me or the world. Yet, I needed the Knight's steadfastness and courage. My future choices might not win any popularity contests – and that was a tough thing to accept given my sensitive nature. My hope was that I would forge ahead, even in the face of criticism.

The lingering question was: Could I return to the retreat the next year, or had that bridge been burned? When registration opened for the following year's event, I went ahead and registered, knowing that my registration might be rejected. And, not surprisingly, I received a phone call from the registrar. After the usual pleasantries, she made herself clear.

"If I allow you to attend this year's retreat, you have to promise me that you and your entire group will take part in all scheduled activities. What happened last year can never happen again."

I swallowed hard, and responded, "I agree. Your request is completely reasonable. I did not foresee what happened last year and it will never happen again. I can tell you that most of the people who were there with me last year will not be returning. And while I cannot control others' behavior, I will be involved, as I have been in the past."

I took a few moments to think about what – if anything – I should add. I decided to proceed, even though my gut was starting to knot up. "If you or anyone on the organizing committee prefers that I no longer attend, I will honor that decision. There is no reason for any of us to be uncomfortable with the situation going forward. I appreciate your call and can withdraw my registration request, if you'd like."

She replied, "You do not need to do that. We just want to make sure that you – and any others who might be with you – understand that this is a retreat for those who will participate in the program. Please let everyone who is planning to attend know this."

"I will, and again thanks for your call. I will see you in September."

After that exchange, I sat for a while, contemplating the situation. Would I be comfortable showing up at the retreat, and how would I be received? As it turned out, I did attend, and while there were some initial awkward moments, by the end of the retreat things were back to normal. The other attendees' forgiveness of me was another valuable lesson.

A Surprise Ending

My Buddhist friends often talk about striving to detach from the outcomes of our actions. They point out that distancing ourselves from expectations and results can help us achieve peace. In principle, this is a wonderful ideal.

I will also admit to being a human. I have hopes and dreams, and when I fully invest myself in something, I do have desired outcomes. The vision of a desired outcome seems to ramp up exponentially when I am in love with someone. Love comes with a projected future when I am part of a committed couple.

After Jen's visit, I began working on the logistics of how our lives could be merged. I dove into the proverbial deep end and prepared myself for the long, hard swim that might be necessary for us to build a relationship. Emotional detachment was the last thing on my mind.

But during phone conversations leading up to our scheduled rendezvous in Florida, I realized the extent of the dilemma that Jen faced. She had attended the previous workshops because of a close friend and mentor. I sensed that our relationship posed a threat to that strong bond. It appeared that Jen might have to choose between me – the potential partner with lots of unknowns – and her current life and relationships. And with two children, she had several considerations to weigh.

I arrived at the conference a day before her. My hopes were sky-high that we might soon begin planning a future together. When she had visited me earlier, it was downright painful to give her a hug and then watch her head into the guest bedroom. I kept thinking that she might change her mind during the upcoming visit, and curl up with me.

When she arrived, I sensed something was wrong. She did not seek contact with me and was standoffish. After about an hour of awkwardness between us, it was time to ask the question.

"Jen, what's going on?"

"I've decided to fly back home. I'm not going to the workshop with you. I realized on the flight that I belong home with my children. I am not willing to change my life. I like it as it is."

The firmness of her tone and the determined look in her eyes made it clear that there was no room for discussion. There was nothing I could say or do that was going to change her mind. Our budding relationship was not to blossom, so I did my best to suck it up and be honorable. We had not made any promises to each other, and she owed me nothing.

While my insides felt shattered and my hopes dashed, revealing those feelings to her would not serve any purpose. Instead, I held on to a faint hope. Perhaps, if I did not try to manipulate her feelings, I thought, we might have a chance down the road. I believed that "this one" was worth the wait. And maybe the prospect of sharing a room was too much pressure, and that forced her into a premature decision.

Honoring her feelings and being as supportive as possible, I wanted to leave the door open for us. Mustering up every bit of strength my Knight possessed, I did my absolute best to offer empathy.

"I understand that you've been pulled in many different directions," I said. "I am deeply saddened by your decision. I believe we had a chance to build something wonderful together. However, I respect that you are trying to do what is best for you and your family. We faced a lot of challenges, and I would have willingly faced them with you. Now I only ask that you not leave my life entirely. I would, if possible, like to remain in your life, even if it is not as your partner."

"Thank you for understanding, and yes, we can remain friends," she replied.

She departed for the airport the next morning before I was even awake. Her side of the room was empty, and my heart was even emptier. Now that she was gone, reality hit me like a sledgehammer. I lay in bed that morning and sobbed. The Knight within felt mortally wounded – and, once again, betrayed. *Why me?* and *Why again?* surfaced. I was angry at having been set up for heartache. Had not my Knight paid his dues? Why had this potential partner come into my life, only to turn away and leave me emotionally broken? Does this strike a chord?

I was unabashedly in love with Jen. I thought I was being realistic about the barriers before us, and I believed with all of my heart that we could overcome them. What I did not see coming was her abrupt change of mind – the one thing that planning and compromise could never resolve. She knew what her life was with her family, her job, and her current friends. Jen did what she felt was best.

While I attempted to maintain contact with her after that, it was for naught. She never directly told me to go away, but over time it became clear that she had moved on. Her young daughter became pregnant, and Jen's focus shifted to her family and managing an unexpected birth. There was no room for me, and my Knight withdrew from the field. It was a losing battle.

Eventually, I realized that this was another opportunity for me to embrace unconditional love. While I was bitterly disappointed, my love was not contingent on her conforming to my expectations. She also confirmed to me that although I was in my 50s, being in love had not changed much from my high school days. I could still experience incredible feelings of wonder. Being in love was not just a long-faded dream.

One interesting aspect of that brief time with Jen was its similarity to some of my other love relationships where I also had the rug pulled out from under me. It was a pattern I did not want to continue to repeat. So, what were these experiences trying to show me about myself?

I decided to do some self-examination to see if I could determine what was going on (see footnote 2). Did I have trust issues, or fear of commitment, or was it something else?

The main cause turned out to be one I would never have suspected. It was a foundational belief that intimate relationships would always end up causing pain and suffering for me. If what I came up with was true, what I viewed as betrayal by my former loves was simply them validating my own belief. Holding on to that belief, consciously or subconsciously, would naturally prevent any fulfilling relationships.

Based on my training, such beliefs can come from multiple levels. Subconscious beliefs can derive from our current lifetime, our "past" lifetimes, our spiritual or soul level, and from our genetic lineage. Often, we do not have an awareness of such beliefs. We only become aware of them by observing the patterns that continue to unfold in our lives.

More Endings

It has often been said that *there is nothing new under the sun*. We all carry programs and patterns of thought and behavior with us, and we often repeat those patterns. Much of what happens in our lives is a replay of what has occurred in other times and places. How often have you experienced something, apparently for the first time, and yet you feel that it is not new?

Our group was about to encounter a *have we been here before?* type of experience.

Upon returning from my professional conference, I organized my house for Kimberly's upcoming workshop

– the one that Jen and I had planned to attend together. I was still struggling to make sense of what had happened between us. However, with guests showing up in just four days, I put on my game face and prepared to play host. I never would have guessed that Jen's departure would foreshadow more endings to come. Damn, relationships can be challenging!

It was great to see everyone so soon after our retreat experience. Early in the weekend, Kimberly led us in exercises to help us dismantle our defense mechanisms. Most of us spend tremendous amounts of energy to avoid our shadow-sides, and her program was designed to get us to expose more of ourselves.

But halfway through our first day, tempers flared in response to Kimberly's probing. One recurring theme was forgiveness – letting go of pain that we perceive others have inflicted upon us. I knew from experience that the victim role could be seductive, especially since I had just gone through the pain of heartbreak. Also, my Knight gave up his life believing that he was the victim of the powers that be – including his God. The modern-day me could easily justify plenty of self-pity, looking at life from the Knight's perspective.

It can be challenging for us to even admit that we have a problem. We must accept our shadow-side before we can heal what is there – and that is painful. Many of us, including yours truly, defend our beliefs – we are sure of our rightness. I have held onto anger and resentment far beyond their usefulness, because I felt justified. It is much easier to blame others than to take responsibility for our own situation.

By the end of the first evening, two camps formed within the workshop. One group agreed with Kimberly's direction, which was to continue digging into those shadow-side aspects of ourselves. Those aspects could be vows, beliefs or attitudes – underlying elements that were holding us back from love. It is never easy to unearth those things buried deep inside our shadow-side or our subconscious.

The other group believed that they were already enlightened, and that Kimberly's intrusion into their beliefs was unjustified. As much as Kimberly did her best to be compassionate, this group viewed her exercises as personal attacks. In one case, a participant screamed, "I will never be vulnerable again and I see no reason to be! This workshop is a complete waste of my time." It was clear that the participants in the second camp were not there to have their beliefs or values challenged.

Emotions further escalated after a one-on-one exercise. The "I am never going to be vulnerable again" person was paired with someone with a shy personality. The purpose of the exercise was to mirror each other, to expose blind spots or hidden weaknesses. So, the now-angry person was looking at someone who reflected her own vulnerability – and she was not happy, not one bit. According to her, the exercise was of no use. She believed that she needed to be with someone as strong as she saw herself to be. The result was an irreparable split.

My reaction to the dissident group was less than positive. If all they were going to do was complain, why were they even there? A part of me just wanted them to leave and stop the disruptions. I believed the rest of us were willing to be open, whereas that group of people was not.

After I got past my initial reactions, watching the scenario play out was fascinating. At one point, I was lying on the floor, petting Sir Fulton and observing as Kimberly moved around the group. She was confronting each of us, one at a time. While I was watching her, an image of Jesus working with his followers surfaced within me. That event also ended up creating factions. I felt a recognition and a deep sadness. Were we destined to play out the same dynamics and experience the same endings? Why could we not learn and move forward together?

As a result of that week, I lost the friendships of a number of people. My first reaction was to see them as wrong and afraid to explore their own vulnerabilities. But if I stopped there with my feelings, I would have missed the key points of a lesson. Why was my ego tied up in their chosen paths? Was I taking my own journey to gain social support or the admiration of others? If that was the case, then I could see that my path was going to lead to more pain and suffering.

The experiences with Jen, along with what happened at the retreat and at the workshop, showed me that surprises were to be expected on my Quest. I could see that I was going to be challenged on every level, and questions would keep coming. Could I love and value those who disagreed with me, criticized me, or disappointed me? Could I learn and grow from such experiences? I still had a long way to go on my Quest of unconditional love. The Knight within had plenty of tarnish on his armor.

YEAR THREE
Looking Back

Now that Dad was gone, I was spending more time with my mother. I created a mini-office at the family home, and all I needed to work there was my laptop computer. It felt like I had two homes and I bounced back and forth between them. In many ways, I felt more emotionally attached to my family home than I did to my own home. As the years were slipping by, I knew that the time of having Mom here on earth, was coming to an end. I tried to enjoy those waning experiences to the fullest.

Throughout the third year, I could feel a momentum building. I appreciated the steadfastness of the Knight inside me, because I would at times need to rely on his strength when things looked bleak. This third year was proof that my chosen path was going to pose significant challenges, whether it meant violating others' expectations or seeing people leave unexpectedly.

My humanness was on full display after losing Jen. No armor or shield was going to protect me from such heartache or the experience of having my hopes dashed. I did, however, do my best to take solace in the fact that I could still fall in love. And, I was shedding vows that had been affecting me for lifetimes.

Source also gave me an opportunity to gauge my progress and experience the incredible power of gratitude. One beautiful Sunday morning, I headed out on a bicycle ride. I was having a spectacular day and was in high spirits. It was sunny, the temperature was perfect, and traffic was on the light side. Even the drivers who passed by me seemed to mirror my excellent mood and were exceptionally courteous. Life was good!

So, what happened next took me totally by surprise.

On my ride back home, I was on a smooth, wide road with a tailwind, which was always a blessing on the ride home. As I approached a street on my right, I noticed a car on my left. The car slowed down to my pace and I figured that the driver was waiting for me to clear the intersection. After 30-plus years of cycling, I could usually sense what a driver was going to do, and I would always respond accordingly. But this time, I did not anticipate what was about to happen.

Without any warning, he turned directly into my path toward the side street, and suddenly I was headed into the car's front passenger door. But miraculously, my bike was pulled to the right, out of harm's way. It was as if a force took over at that moment. I have no idea how I did not slam directly into that car.

I have to admit that I yelled less-than-kind words as the driver sped away – like I did not exist. Usually in a situation like this, the Knight in me, and the "me" in most of this lifetime, would have gone after the driver. I typically would have been blind with rage about how the stupid driver could have seriously injured me.

Instead, I immediately got off the road to let the adrenaline rush subside and to steady myself. While I was not happy about what the driver had done, the intense anger I normally would have felt was absent. I was shocked that I had not collided with the car and relieved that I was not waiting for an ambulance.

Once I settled down and stopped shaking, I resumed my ride home. A couple of miles later, I was overwhelmed with a sense of gratitude. I knew, on some level, that there had been an intervention on my behalf. As I spoke to whatever or whoever had come to my aid in that split second, I felt an incredible connection take place. I was completely overcome with emotion and quickly pulled off the road again. I slumped over my handlebars and cried. I must have been a sight, standing off on the side of the road and crying uncontrollably. I think I was releasing the emotions of the experience, but it felt like much more. It was like gratitude was finally deeply rooted within me as part of who I am.

I was hoping that maybe – just maybe – Year Three would be the high-water mark for challenges. So much had happened, and I felt I was making progress toward whatever I was meant to learn and do. However, as in previous years, I did not anticipate what was coming. Sometimes it is a gift not knowing that the light at the end of the tunnel is really an oncoming train.

YEAR FOUR

The Dragon and the Dark Night

Spring

My Elusive Dragon

Following Jen's departure from my life and the splintering of the group, I expected my life to go back to some semblance of normal. I focused on my job, took care of Sir Fulton, exercised, and did the everyday stuff of life. I had come through some tough challenges and deserved a respite.

I was about to experience the opposite.

I discovered that I had moved into a role with the remaining group members that would test me – and them – in ways I could never have imagined. My mission was like that of a knight taking on a fire-breathing dragon or going in search of the Holy Grail. It is the nature of knights to accept missions that do not make much sense. While I understood that foolish tendency, I never dreamt that I would play a role that would make a fire-breathing dragon look friendly or an endless quest seem like a vacation. It would be my **dark night of the soul**.

We all experience times when we feel challenged far beyond our capabilities to cope. At those times, we may even consider an exit from our physical lives. But such an exit would only forestall what we need to face. When we allow ourselves to open to who and what we truly are – eternal and divine beings – the dark night of the soul can often be part of the growth experience. The question is whether we can come through our dark night with a greater understanding of why we chose to walk such a difficult path.

During the fourth year of our group working together, I received a call from Kimberly. "I have something I need to tell you," she said, "but I do not want you to feel like you are being attacked." Her usual light-hearted tone was conspicuously absent.

At that point, my heart rate accelerated; I knew something heavy was coming.

"OK, what is it?"

"There are some in the group that feel their energy is being taken from them. They sense it is from a connection at the root chakra and they are being drained. They also believe, as do I, that you are the one doing it."

I was gut-punched. Words failed me. I tried to calm myself without much success. How could I respond to that? How could I be unknowingly harming loved ones?

A lot of possible reasons for Kimberly's call had raced through my mind moments earlier, but this one was not on the list. My intention had always been to support the group members as much as I could.

"Are you OK?" she finally asked.

Finding my voice, I stuttered, "I don't know what to say." And, damn straight, I felt attacked.

"There must be something in you that feels you have to do this," she replied. "You do not have to say anything right now. I trust you will figure out what is going on."

"Can you give me any idea why you think this is occurring?"

"My sense is that you feel you need to do this to survive. But, this is critical for you to figure out on your own."

We ended the call and I sat in stunned silence. *What the hell just happened?*

Given the close relationships that our group members had developed with me in our many workshops together, including one-on-one work, I did not think to question what they were experiencing. I also concluded that it was valid, since it was my mentor, Kimberly, who was passing on the information. So, I began the search for what inside of me might be causing others harm.

At first, the best explanation I could come up with was that my occasional bouts of low energy might be causing me to unconsciously draw energy from the others. I entertained the real possibility that the energy drain was in fact my fault. My first response to that thought was to ramp up my efforts to do no harm and to connect with Source energy. I worked hard not to vilify or condemn myself – something I had been a master of in this lifetime, and probably in others as well.

In my saner moments, I did my best to appreciate that no matter what I had done, or was doing, it had helped me arrive at this place of understanding. Awareness is the first step in positive change, and I was definitely aware of a problem. This latest development challenged me to accept even more of my shadow-side – the place where we wall off those things we fear.

In my less-sane moments, I experienced intense emotional pain. The group that I looked to for spiritual support was accusing me of doing something against them, and that tapped into my tendency towards self-recrimination. I understood why so much ends up in our shadow-side – some things are just too damn painful to face.

With what courage I could muster, I looked at the situation and focused on shifting whatever was necessary.

I vowed to derive energy only from Source or Mother Earth, and to do no harm. I found it ironic that I was making a new vow, after having suffered so much from past vows. But I did not take this new one lightly. Before taking that leap of faith, I intuitively checked to see if taking the new vow was in accord with my highest good. Every indication was positive, and so I made the vow.

With my stronger connection to Source, I hoped that my days of causing problems for others were over. For a while, life was quiet and I took this as a positive sign. The calm, however, did not last – I was, after all, on a Quest.

I was doing healing sessions via telephone with one of my fellow group members. One afternoon, I received an angry phone call from him. He proclaimed that I was enacting "energetic rape." He was sure that I was attacking him, and he demanded that it stop. My friend now saw me as a threat to his well-being and was severing all contact with me. The gut-punched feeling was back – in spades. I would have loved to stop whatever it was that I was accused of doing – if only I had a clue as to how.

I went into a complete emotional freefall. What was happening? Why was I harming those whom I loved and trusted? I was actually beginning to not trust myself.

What in my shadow-side was so insidious that I could not resolve it? I promised myself that I would persevere in my search. This had to stop!

I spent the next few days exploring every avenue and nuance that came to mind. Except for my accuser, the others in the group continued to support me because they knew I was not drawing energy from them on a conscious level. Yet, not even Kimberly knew how to help me. She was convinced that this dilemma was something I needed to face on my own.

But what the hell was it? I was isolated and scared – especially of myself. I felt as if I was wandering aimlessly in a spiritual desert, with no oasis in sight. The rejection from those who had become my tribe pervaded both my sleep and my waking hours. I was an emotional wreck. My ability to focus was shot to hell.

Up to that point, I thought I understood the shadow. For instance, if greed is in our shadow, we might avoid it by being generous or philanthropic. We often do the opposite of what is in our shadow in order to counteract it.

Even with that understanding, to have a shadow that harmed others was abhorrent to me. I vacillated among feelings of despair, defeat, and denial. Every time my mind wandered back to my dilemma, it felt like a fist hit my solar plexus, and my anxiety flared.

The struggle became even more poignant when the person who believed that I was causing him harm demanded my removal from our spiritual group. While that added more hurt to the mix, I could not blame him for wanting me gone. I assured the others that I would not rest until I had the issue under control. My words, of course, did not mollify the individual who was opposed to my presence in the group. Because the others refused to exile me, we lost him as a member.

During that period, Kimberly continued to offer what emotional support she could. She encouraged me to increase my efforts to address the problem, and assured me that she had faith in me. I took action by spending more time in meditation. While meditating, I asked – and sometimes pleaded – to be shown what exactly was happening. And, whenever I felt something spiritually objectionable come forward to be healed or shifted, I used the theta technique on it (footnote 1).

Despite my efforts, my inner dragon remained elusive. I only knew it by its smoldering aftermath – its harmful effects on others. What was it, and where was it hiding?

My Knight was at a complete loss. It is one thing to confront one's fears when the foe is plainly visible. What does one do when the foe is unfathomable?

I focused on connecting with Source, and shifted anything that might cause me to take others' energy. I reinforced, on every level, my belief in the sovereignty of every individual and their right to their own life-force energy. However, throughout all of my digging and exploring, nothing surfaced that would explain what was causing the issue. There was no big "Aha!" moment of discovery or engagement – no triumphant moment where I stood over my vanquished dragon.

While continuing the search for my dragon, life returned to semi-normal. The one significant exception was my decision to wind down my academic career. A number of factors contributed to the decision. My teaching had spanned 30 years; my final doctoral student was finishing up her degree; a milestone had been achieved in my research; and I was encouraged to take on more administrative duties – my version of hell. I sensed that there were changes ahead.

As spring was waning, Kimberly suggested that group members pair up via telephone and refocus on core challenges. I had a new partner, and we did healing work together over the phone. I took this success as a sign of being accepted back into the group. During this time, my dragon went dormant. I hoped that the spiritual work I was doing had vanquished my inner beast. Maybe the dragon had been a constellation of challenges, and therefore difficult to pinpoint.

Such optimism did not last long. One afternoon, Kimberly called to tell me that my pattern of taking energy from others had reemerged. "I hate to tell you this, but others have contacted me saying that you are stealing their energy, again," she said.

A knife went into my gut and twisted at the word "again." I was now a repeat offender. Why had I not been able to stop this? What in the world was this dragon, and how could I find it? Could I ever defeat it?

I replied, "Kimberly, once again, I do not know what to say. I have done everything I can think of – I do not know what else to do. I have pleaded with Source to guide me. Why is this still happening?"

"I wish I could tell you."

"Can you help me? Please!" I was pleading for my life.

"I am as baffled as you are, and I do not believe anyone can help you, but you. This is something you need to figure out."

I felt a black hole open up beneath me. An anxious depression set in, gnawing at me from the inside. I pushed my physical workouts to the limit in a desperate attempt to gain some peace. But I was afraid of myself, which left no place to run. Would there be any way for me to go back to the group, or to the spiritual path that was the basis of my identity?

I soon reached the low point of my struggles. My nerves were shot and I began to contemplate suicide. I was failing in my vow to do no harm. What was this monster? Could I find release in death? The disquieting thought was: *No.* I would have to face this dragon now, or it would resurface in other lifetimes. How do you vanquish a dragon when it is you, and when even choosing death is not the answer?

During the two weeks that followed my conversation with Kimberly, I did not hear from any group members. My feelings of abandonment intensified. These people, whom I relied upon for my spiritual and emotional support, were telling me I was evil. I was a pariah in their eyes. My sleep became ever more fitful, and I withdrew further into myself. I was even afraid of what people in my normal life might see in me.

One night, as I headed to bed, I admitted that it was time I bid farewell to the group. I would make a decision about taking my life later. In that moment, a sense of resolve came over me, and a glimmer of hope shone through the wreckage of my ravaged emotional state.

An interesting thing happened once I gave voice to my decision. I became aware that we, as a group, had faced this same scenario in the past. At that moment, I remembered my conversation with Kimberly from the workshop when my Knight first appeared. She had told me that I had removed myself from the group for many lifetimes.

If that was true, this heartbreaking riddle had followed me through time! Now I was desperate! What the hell was I up against that plagued me, lifetime after lifetime? Did I have a chance of healing it now, or was I doomed to cause unintentional harm to others for lifetimes to come? An answer emerged that evening during my meditation.

I relax into my breath and focus on my connection with Source. I plead for help from Source and my guides with my dilemma. I receive the message that everything is fine and that I am on the right path. I try to absorb this response and to settle the utter chaos swirling in me. Try as I might to believe it, absolutely nothing feels fine. What the bloody hell am I missing?

Archangel Michael stands before me and I hear, "You are the test." Feeling frustrated, I shoot back, "What the hell do you mean by the test?" He answers my question lovingly with a question that rocks my world: "How have you liked playing the Judas role for your group?" I respond, "It sucks!"

I lay on my bed, trying to sort out what it all meant. Why was I playing such a role? Why did the group need a Judas?

Over the next few days, many of the pieces fell into place. In contrast to the biblical portrayal of Judas, I had never believed he was a traitor. I had always thought, *How does one betray someone who can foresee the future, calm storms, walk on water, and raise the dead?* My conclusion was that it was not possible.

Some accounts of Judas depict him as the one who understood Jesus's choice of crucifixion. Therefore, Judas agreed to do the unthinkable. The sad part is that the biblical Judas never forgave himself, and he committed suicide. I understood and identified with him – my guilt had me considering the exact same fate.

I had not forgiven myself for taking on a role that challenged the others at the core of their existence. But it went further than that. I had not forgiven the group, either, for the many lifetimes where I was compelled to live apart from them. There were huge wounds to heal. The key questions were: Why did I accept the Judas role, and what purpose did it serve?

During a meditation a few days later, I thought about how the disciples must have reacted to Judas after Jesus's arrest and crucifixion. Jesus taught love, and his crucifixion taught the lesson of everlasting life and unconditional love. But, after the crucifixion, I will bet it was not unconditional love that the disciples demonstrated toward Judas. He represented the things about ourselves that we reject – he represented our shadow.

Jesus's sacrifice was meant to teach us about unconditional love and forgiveness. The message: If we can forgive those who we believe have done the unthinkable, then we have learned the truth about unconditional love.

For whatever reason, I had agreed to help the group, and myself, learn that same lesson. They believed that I was the traitor who turned on them. To the disciples and the vast majority of those who follow the Christian faith, Judas betrayed Christ. To my group, I had violated their feelings of sovereignty and sapped their energy. What could be more personal?

I now had a handle on something that had affected me over many lifetimes. Was it time for all of us to heal? When I used my intuition to ask Source, I received confirmation that my job was finished – and that the true healing could begin.

After all that had happened, I needed to forgive myself and the others; the former action seemed like it would be the biggest hurdle. But the tremendous anger within me would prove to have many layers.

The patterns we build into the fabric of our being over many lifetimes can be difficult to release. These patterns, which are formed by powerful emotions and beliefs, influence our personalities at the subconscious level. Undoing such pervasive aspects of myself would take time, effort and persistence.

Why had this dragon remained hidden for so long? Upon reflection, it seemed to me that I needed to have time in my own spiritual desert. *Who was I? Who would I turn to when all seemed lost?* My dragon within forced me to rely less on others and to strengthen my connection with the Divine – the Source of all love. I had previously relied a great deal on Kimberly, my mentor. Now, it was time for me – more than ever – to forge my own journey. The journey was mine – period.

While my role was to forgive the members of the group, those in the group also played essential roles for me. Along with taking responsibility for my journey, they challenged me to embrace the power of love, forgiveness, and gratitude. When those elements are present, there is no room for anger or hate. I admit, it took significant soul-searching for me to appreciate what it took for the other group members to play their parts in our multi-lifetime drama.

My Knight's Quest of self-discovery has been akin to a voyage through the land of Oz, with surprises at every turn. In the story, Dorothy had to face almost insurmountable perils and do things she could never have imagined in her wildest dreams. Yet, when she awoke from what seemed to be a dream, she had a fresh perspective on her life and an appreciation for all that life included. She took the hero's journey and was renewed by her adventures.

It was the same for me.

By coming through this last experience, I realized that there was a strength within me that would enable me to face my life in a different way – with a greater sense of self-empowerment. That self-empowerment pushed me to look less to others for my identity and spiritual direction. I learned – as others have – that while we can welcome help and support, ultimately, we are on a quest of self-discovery that is ours and ours alone.

From medieval battlefields to energetic and spiritual realms, my Knight continued to forge ahead in his Quest to understand the true essence of love and forgiveness. Did it need to be so hard? I asked that question when Jen left, and again when I was pushed from the nest of my spiritual group. It seems that I was, and probably still am, prone to doing things the hard way.

I could only guess that on some level, I had decided to bring a variety of difficult experiences into my life. Fortunately, I had created a life structure that was functioning well; I had a good career, a home, and a faithful, furry companion. I was able to set aside time to face challenges that transcended centuries. My Knight stood ready to shift my focus from the outward world of accomplishments to the inner world of my Ultimate Quest.

Years Later

The Knights Templar

During the process of revising this book, a friend provided feedback. She had some comments about the episode involving my Judas role; she challenged me to look further into what took place during Jesus's time and why I perceived that it ended in tragedy. It did not take me long to better understand why she pushed me to probe more deeply.

Many times during this lifetime, I felt that I was conducting my life according to the highest good, and playing by the appropriate rules – and yet, things ended badly. I decided that I needed to understand if there was a common theme. So, during a meditation, I asked for additional clarity.

A scene arose before me that involved the Knights Templar. From what I understand, they created the first banking system, protected the monarchy, and were faithful to the church. One day, soldiers burst in and arrested them. They were jailed, tortured into making false confessions, and many were burned at the stake. History suggests that the reason for what happened to them was because the King was indebted to them, and because the Church judged them to be too powerful. They were a threat.

As that scene arose for me to review, I experienced an extreme visceral reaction to what happened to the knights. I could taste my anger and horror over the betrayal. I asked in the meditation if I carried energy from those times of the Templars; I received a "yes."

That long-ago scene was another possible situation where I – or at least some aspect of me – experienced suffering while trying to do what I thought was noble. If we carry emotional scars or beliefs based on trauma from other times, we can continue to validate them – lifetime after lifetime – while being unaware of their origin. We can subconsciously expect the worst, regardless of our intentions. We can recreate similar, unwanted outcomes, time and again.

How many of us have felt that no matter how hard we try to do the "right thing," something goes wrong? Are we carrying emotional scars that we continue to validate?

Summer

Many Times, Many Places?

It never ceases to amaze me how seemingly insignificant events can lead to a new insight. We see something that catches our attention and we end up taking a different route home, or we observe others' behavior and it suddenly changes our perspective.

Such an event occurred one day when two well-dressed young men rang my doorbell. A glance out of my upstairs window made me think that they were Mormons doing their required missionary work, so I decided not to answer. I saw that they lingered for a few minutes, and then moved on to my neighbor's house.

But the young men at my door that day inspired an interesting train of thought. Instead of dismissing the incident, I started thinking about the history of religion, and the tendency that humans have to believe that they are right and everyone else is wrong. While disputes over resources or territory have always occurred, disagreements over religious ideologies have been a primary reason for countless conflicts. Why is this? Most religious faiths profess love and acceptance – so how do they become mired in conflict?

While mulling over that dilemma, images from a few of my earthly lifetimes flowed through my mind. It was doubtful that I ever practiced the same religion or spirituality in any two lifetimes. And in the world today, many religions exist, each providing a different perspective and experience. Since our nationality, race and family often determine our religious practices or spiritual perspectives, is it possible that, for each lifetime, we choose the religion that we most need to grow?

It is easy to disregard others' spiritual practices as stupid, destructive, or evil. For example, a former girlfriend believed that my books on Edgar Cayce were demonic; predictably, it was a short-lived relationship.

Thanks to those young men at my door, I began to consider that every spiritual perspective has potential benefits. Life on earth is the ultimate buffet, with limitless options. What a bountiful learning environment!

This led to the thought: *What if?* What would happen if we stopped investing our time, effort and resources to try to prove that others are wrong? How would things change if we saw everyone's various spiritual practices as just something that those individuals need to experience in this lifetime? Have I experienced the totality of being a devout Mormon, Quaker, Hasidic Jew, Muslim, Hindu, Buddhist or Catholic? I am sure the answer is no.

Why, then, do we debate, disparage, or disdain those who do not agree with our religious practices? Why did I – the Knight – take to the battlefield and fly the banner of Christ, believing that I was doing God's will? I think it is because the Knight believed that we only get one shot at a pleasant afterlife. If we believe – as he did – that we are on the correct path to the afterlife, those who do not share our beliefs are, by definition, wrong or misguided.

The Knight in me who went forth to battle believed that his version of spirituality was the only one. His salvation was riding on that single lifetime. Considering the pitfalls he faced, his struggle was like a golfer getting only one swing at a hole-in-one! The Knight was trying to prove he was right, and worthy of being blessed by his judgmental God. He also believed that he needed to "save" others – even if it meant killing them.

Do we really have only one shot? Most western religions say yes. That perspective posed a problem for the young me as I sat in church. Our church, what I would label as liberal Presbyterian, taught that salvation depends on being a good, kind and generous person. These same principles are embraced by many religions.

On Sundays, we heard about people in need who did not have enough to sustain themselves or were living in horrendous, subhuman conditions. I can still remember the flood of refugees that came through our town in the 1950s as they fled the expanding Soviet Union.

I felt badly for those people and made a donation from my allowance. But something kept gnawing at me, and it had to do with God. How could a loving, compassionate God let those refugees live in squalid or repressive conditions, when I was living in a middle-class home with plenty to eat? With such inequity to begin with, how could we be striving for the same outcome in a single lifetime? None of it felt fair, even for me as a child.

Later in life, I found out that the concept of individuals having experienced multiple lifetimes on earth was not a far-fetched belief. Edgar Cayce did past-life readings beginning in the 1920s; and religions with millions of followers – such as Buddhism and Hinduism – believe in reincarnation. The possibility exists that we have had many lives on earth and that we learn, grow and make discoveries in each one.

If we indeed live on this earth many times, how might that belief change our views of life, death, good and evil? What happens if what we discover during each lifetime stays with us for future ones? I came to believe that the Knight, who could not have conceived of such a possibility, was gaining a different perspective on earthly life through his current embodiment – me.

So, why was my lifetime as a knight so central to my current journey? Why would that particular lifetime be the one to capture my attention? Why should the Knight's lifetime be the touchstone on my Quest to understand love? Maybe, because in that lifetime, I was willing to sacrifice my life instead of living a lie. My faith had been shattered, and my life had lost its meaning. In many ways, that lifetime was a spiritual rock bottom; there was nothing left to lose. Yet, from that place, my Ultimate Quest emerged. Sometimes we need to lose it all before we can create a new path forward.

Return to the Mountain

My Quest continued to show me that our subconscious mind is powerful. It can often run our lives, without us being aware of what is actually happening. But how could I let go of my shadow-side elements, when I did not even know what I was holding on to? I was about to receive a powerful demonstration of how to find what is hiding in the subconscious. In my case, I had to take on a mountain to find out.

Two years earlier, during Jen's visit, she and I climbed a mountain and watched the turkey vultures. Since that mountain was over an hour's drive from my home, I had not ventured back there since our hike to the top. That changed when I attended a gathering that was scheduled to be held at the mountain's base.

When the day of the event arrived, I finished up my Sir Fulton dog duties and headed to the event. When I arrived, I could not find the group. So, I circled the entire mountain hoping to spot them. As I passed the lot where Jen and I parked to ascend the mountain, I somehow knew I needed to return to the summit. I sensed that a climb to the top was the real reason I was there.

I finally found the gathering a few minutes later and enjoyed a few hours with the group. As the event concluded, I headed back to the trailhead parking lot. The clouds were thickening, and I recalled there was a forecast for thunderstorms. After checking with my intuitive guidance, I grabbed the small umbrella that lived in my car and began my hike upward.

I had gone two-thirds of the way up the mountain when I heard distant thunder. I asked my intuitive guidance: *Is this venture really necessary?* "Yes," was the clear answer. *Damn,* I thought. I hiked on. As the clouds darkened and the thunder grew louder, I doubted my sanity. Everyone else in the area was retreating down the mountain.

The top of the mountain was bare of any vegetation. What was left of my logical self, which was not much, knew that it was a dangerous place in a thunderstorm. *Is it time to run back to the parking lot?* I asked. I knew the answer was "No!"

The lightning was close by, and a heavy, cold rain began, driven by strong wind gusts. Even with the umbrella, my lower half became drenched. I told Source that if this was the time for me to leave my body, I had a few requests. *Please have someone discover that Fulton is home alone and make sure he has a loving family,* I thought. (This was before I had a cellular phone.) My overriding concern was for my furry companion. *Also, can the lightning strike take me quickly?* I asked. I had no desire for prolonged suffering.

I was cold, soggy and disgruntled when I arrived at the mountaintop visitors' center. I asked Source if the weather would be clear enough for me to descend the mountain safely. I received a "yes" to that question, and noticed the rain letting up as the sky lightened on the horizon.

Why am I up here? Leaving the visitors' center, I walked over to where Jen and I had watched the vultures ride the thermals. As I looked out over the scene we had experienced together, minus Jen and the vultures, my heart felt heavy. I realized there was an emptiness inside that I had been ignoring. God, I missed her.

In a silent prayer, I asked, *Dear Source, please lift these emotions from me.* Moments later, the sadness subsided. Next, I asked, *Could this healing have occurred in a less dramatic way?* The humorous response was, "No, or you'd have done it already."

So, again I was reminded that we need to recognize an issue before we can heal it or release it. The journey down the mountain was uneventful. Much to my amusement, during the entire drive home from the mountain, the sun was shining brightly. Maybe the rain represented the tears I was ignoring? Once again, it seemed I needed to do things the hard way. Maybe it was time to change my pattern.

Climbing a mountain in a storm should have stressed me out. What allowed me to ascend the mountain calmly in those conditions? Maybe I had learned to trust Source; was this a turning point for my inner Knight in his relationship with God?

Facing such a trial helped me gain a greater connection with my Knight's steadfastness, even when it did not make logical sense. While he gave up his life on that battlefield, he never abandoned his Ultimate Quest. Death was not the end he imagined it would be, and so he had reemerged in that workshop with me three years ago. I had given him the opening to enter my life, and it changed both of us forever.

Fall

Integrating the Sword

I was on the verge of learning a lesson from the Sword – which, for me, symbolized tremendous power. Its initial appearance felt like pure power as its energy surged through my body, and later it channeled pure love, vanquishing the angry monster within me. Thanks to the Sword, I was able to learn that such energy does not come from external things, but resides inside of us.

Since it first appeared, the Sword was a sacred symbol containing what I believed to be a power far surpassing my own. I felt that it had its own energy – energy that I was privileged to wield. That idea of separate energy was about to change, thanks to what would be our group's last workshop with Kimberly. She was ready to push us forward to our grand finale and we eagerly anticipated the experience.

As we approached the end of Year Four, our group now numbered six. Kimberly was living in San Antonio, Texas, and we met at her home. Early in our workshop,

Kimberly explained how the power of love lives in each of us. Then, during one of our discussions, Kimberly placed the sword she had gifted me in front of her. Thinking about what she was teaching us, I gazed at the physical sword in front of her. I asked, "Why do I always imagine the sword doing the work, if the true power of love resides within?"

"The Sword has been your symbol of power for a very long time," Kimberly responded.

A door of understanding flew open. As long as I denied the power within me, I realized, the Sword's energy would remain an external force. It was the Sword's power and not mine. I could remain safely in the background, taking neither responsibility nor credit for what occurred – and would occur – with the Sword.

I could see that the time had come for me to claim the Sword's power as my own. I used the workshop's evening meditation to do just that.

I focus on my breath and visualize the Sword before me. I concentrate on its brilliant, radiant essence of love. The Sword's image becomes more intense, and I see it as I did when it first appeared. It points skyward, with its blade emblazoned in light. I will it to come toward me, and I experience its sheer power. My chest expands to encompass its energy. Its light spreads throughout my entire being. I watch it dissolve within me. The Sword and I are one.

Until that meditation, the Sword's pure love felt unobtainable. Now I was being called to carry its energy. There was a subtle, but discernible, shift in me – a knowing that within each of us there lives a power beyond what we can imagine. A new enthusiasm flooded me. With love's vitality finally inside of me instead of just in the Sword, I felt more certain of following my Quest – wherever it would lead. I hoped for no more dark nights of the soul – the last one almost finished me.

A week after the workshop, I sensed that there was another aspect of the Sword for me to discover. While the Sword represented the power of love, there was something else there too. I again turned to meditation, the tool that had been the foundation of my Quest:

I ask that the deeper dimension of the Sword be revealed. A dense fog appears before me. An image of the Sword is cutting through it. Where its blade moves, light shines through, and its meaning hits me. The Sword of love has the power to cut through our illusions. Thus, we have the ability – using the same power of love – to see through life's fog. Love is not only a power, but a way to view the world.

At that point, I believed that the workshops with Kimberly had come to an end and that I had reconciled my role as the group's Judas. And following Jen's departure, I was back on my own, and expected that life would be more normal.

Once again, I was mistaken.

YEAR FOUR
Looking Back

The good news from Year Four is that I survived. My dragon had been laid to rest. I had been changed by the struggle. My hope was that I had been forged anew, with a stronger connection to Source and to my spiritual guides.

Maybe the most critical shift for my Knight was that love, the ultimate salve for the pain he felt, was inside of him – and by extension, inside of me. He and I understood that love was not something given by an external source or to hold in our hands, like the Sword. It was, in fact, already part of our essential nature.

In my professional life, my colleagues and I were having success in publishing our organizational change research in some of the top professional journals, and the colleague who had invited me to join the project was going to retire at the end of the year. To cap his career, he wanted to publish a book that would summarize what we discovered. It was groundbreaking because our conclusions went against how change management was being taught. I agreed that a book was an excellent idea, and we began to work on it and look for a publisher.

It was fulfilling to bring together what we had learned from our change research. It would not be another book filled with anecdotal stories of change, successes and failures. Instead, we had data that pointed to some of the classic mistakes that organizations make during change initiatives.

While contacting publishers, we were surprised to find that some of the most notable companies were not interested. We received some interesting responses; it turned out that our findings challenged a number of "sacred cows" or top-selling authors in the field. Our data disputed what had become accepted as fact. Entrenched beliefs are difficult to dislodge on any level – personal, organizational, or societal.

It was another lesson that we do not become heroes or credible teachers just by having valuable information. Sometimes it is easier for the audience to shoot the messenger than it is to rethink a longstanding position.

Finally, we were fortunate to gain a sympathetic ear with Stanford University Press. With its help, we proceeded to publish our book. The book was, in many ways, the highlight of Year Four. The achievement set the tone for my professional life for the year.

But the way students wanted to learn was changing. My teaching method had been based on a high level of interaction with students; I expected them to be in class and to take an active part in discussions. It was the only way I knew to convey knowledge that went beyond just memorization. My students, however, wanted all of my notes and materials posted, so that showing up for class would be optional.

It was during Year Four when I admitted to myself that my frustration was increasing and my motivation to teach was waning. At the end of the year, I applied for a partial leave of absence to assess my life and my options

YEAR FIVE

Love and the Quest

Spring

Stepping Up

As it turned out, our fall workshop had an unexpected sequel; Kimberly decided to do one more workshop in Year Five. She felt that there were a few more steps we could take together before we each branched out on our own. We readily accepted, and once again came together in San Antonio.

The first day of our workshop proved to be most important for me. Kimberly began the session by saying there was a group, in spirit, waiting for each of us. It was a message she had received in her meditations while she was seeking guidance for our group.

She instructed us to connect with the highest level of love that we could, and meet those who would be awaiting us. I was skeptical, but did my best to put aside my doubts and allow whatever I was meant to experience. It did not take long.

I am standing in front of a group. I sense their large numbers, rather than see them in any detail. I hear a voice from the crowd, asking if I am ready to fulfill my purpose. I respond that I am, but I admit my hesitation. Fear springs up in my gut about what my purpose might demand.

A ring of fire forms around me. I stand still; the flames move in to fill the circle and engulf my entire energy body. The flames fill me and extend out a few feet around my entire body. The flames are not painful, or even hot.

It is pure light appearing as flames. I know they are there to clear away those things within me that are keeping me from stepping forward. The fire flickers and goes out. A dome of blue energy takes its place. The intuitive message I receive is that the flames can free me of the many beliefs that no longer serve me, and that I should reignite them when I need them.

Returning my focus to the assembled group before me, I sense that they are ready to follow me to the ends of creation. I mount the white stallion that materializes at my side. Everyone else also mounts up, and we head out. As we ride, I know that my role is to lead others to their truest nature – love.

We travel for some time and finally arrive at the Source of pure love. I dismount and I find myself in the presence of a brilliant light that is beyond description. I request help in fulfilling my mission, as I feel overwhelmed by my calling to lead this group in love. I experience Source's energy flow *into my chest and there is tremendous heat as my chest expands. The energy subsides, and I am both emboldened and humbled. I bow in gratitude.*

I turn toward the group that accompanies me. They are on one knee in a show of respect, and as I bow to them, my tears flow. Kimberly is calling us back. I pull myself out of this realm, but I would love to remain.

When we came back to our regular consciousness, we took turns sharing our journeys. As I recounted my experiences, tears were flowing, and I could barely get the words out. Humbled and elated, I was sure of one thing: the group I had encountered was waiting to assist humankind.

Kimberly then had us go back into meditation to our respective journeys so that we could receive any other potential information. I experienced complete humility and gratitude, and felt ready to take my place in humankind's ascendency. What came next was surpris-ing: it was as if a voice other than my own was speaking inside my head.

"We welcome you, our brother and friend. You have journeyed far and wide to grow, learn and discover in order to be ready to return to us. Our hearts sing, now that your

energies are once again with us. We have felt your absence, yet we honored your need to strike out to reclaim your sovereignty. We rejoice that you have rejoined us – forged anew. Our love and assistance will support your every endeavor, and you need never be alone. You have let us into your consciousness and we are here for you, always and forever.

We have much to do. Creation is entering a new stage. You will be with us on our adventures, but we understand you have your own mission. Fear not to venture on your own when called. We connect forever in love and purpose. Ride forth, loving Knight, for more awaits your stepping forward than you can believe."

The focus of the message then turned from me to the entire workshop group:

"Your lives will change in miraculous ways. Do not become lost in the drama. Live, love, and be the joyous beings you are. We stand by you with love, strength and assistance. Blessings from your brothers and sisters."

As I shared these words with the group, I reached for the tissue box. These were tears of joy.

On the last day of the workshop, we discussed what might be holding us back from opening our hearts and stepping into our power. There were a few limiting emotions and beliefs that most of us shared.

Within our group, one commonly-held feeling was the fear of revealing ourselves. We had lived many lives trying to avoid harm; therefore, we tried to fit in and appear normal. Since my Knight had emerged, I realized that much of what made me reluctant to embrace my spiritual purpose involved not wanting to stand out. My instinct was for self-preservation; above all, I wanted to avoid the ire of others.

Because of our past experiences, many of us have feared betrayal or abandonment. Through many lifetimes, we have experienced countless heartaches – and so we have worked to hide or minimize our vulnerability.

The unfortunate result? We keep love at bay. I now understand that love is never lost; however, we can hide from it. We often respond to present-day situations by reliving our pains, hurts and fears. Traumatic events can shape our identities and cause us to view everything through those filters. We end up frozen in a place that we perceive as loveless. As a result, many of us focus on others' needs, while deriving joy from our honorable sacrifices. We avoid facing our pain or examining ourselves. We do not look at how we need to heal. It is easier to work on fixing others than to delve into our own dark places.

The final part of that weekend workshop with Kimberly was an initiation to help us further open our hearts. She worked with us, one at a time, to awaken even more to love. For me, it was a wonderful experience.

I am lying on her massage table with my eyes closed. Kimberly instructs me to relax and be open. Jesus and I are walking down a white path together. He tells me that He will always be with me on my journey. I drink in His love, and gratitude overtakes me. Thanking all of the people who have played significant roles in my life, I envision family, friends, teachers – and tormentors – and I reflect on how important they have been in my life. Filled with tremendous joy, I hear Kimberly telling me to end my journey.

What If It Is You?

With all of the adventures and misadventures I had experienced on my Quest, I started to wonder whether I still desired a partner. I was coming to the conclusion that maybe spiritual journeys are meant to be solo. After all, partnerships can be difficult, even in the best of times.

Maybe it is unrealistic to expect to have someone that close, I thought. *Navigating the twists and turns of a spiritual journey, along with the ups and downs of a personal relationship, might be impossible.* Many great spiritual masters through the ages had remained unattached, so maybe that would be best for me too.

After Jen's departure, I felt more and more that moving forward on my own was simply the way my life was meant to unfold. I felt I had always done my best to make relationships work, but they had always ended. As has often been said, doing something over and over again and expecting different results is insanity.

But yet again, just as I became comfortable with an "insight," it was about to be challenged. There was a woman who had been in my life for more than 10 years. When Kayla and I first met, I felt like I had been hit by the proverbial truck. My reaction occurred before I even really noticed what she looked like or knew anything about her.

Kayla was athletic – she was an aerobics instructor and personal trainer – and had dusty blond hair down to the middle of her back. But she projected a beauty that went far beyond the physical. I also learned that she was a single mom, raising three children – a girl and two boys.

Over the years, a wonderful friendship developed between us. Twice we tried dating, but to no avail. Both times, she admitted, even though she tried, she could not share my feelings. She was not even comfortable holding my hand.

I was simply grateful that she was willing to try. As much as I was attracted to her, I contented myself with our friendship. And, over time, it deepened. We attended an occasional workshop together and enjoyed conversations over dinner every so often. And not long after Jen's departure, Kayla became a member of our spiritual group.

We both resided in the Atlanta area, and for years, Kayla had told me about her home and family in South Carolina. In the spring of Year Five of my Quest, Kayla surprised me; she invited me to visit her family home while she was there. I suspected that she invited me because both her father and brother were facing major health problems and she needed some emotional support. I was traveling at the time, and going to the South Carolina coast on my way home would not be much of a detour.

When I arrived there on a Friday afternoon, I found that her parents' home was at the end of a long gravel road. The entire property was a place of solitude, shrouded in a canopy of trees. I met Valerie, her mom, and Michael, her dad. The house was on a tidal river and the setting was spectacular, with Spanish moss hanging from many of the trees. The marsh began 50 yards behind the house. A long, weathered pier stretched out into the river. The entire scene harkened back to the bygone days of the old South. I could not shake the feeling that the setting was familiar.

From the start of my visit, my original attraction to Kayla came back in full force. I did my best to keep from falling in love with her all over again, since there had been no sign from her that her feelings for me had changed. It was not on my agenda to screw up our incredible friendship by reintroducing possibilities that we put aside years ago.

In bed on Saturday night, I pleaded with Source to help me adjust my feelings toward her. My renewed attraction could endanger our relationship, and could very likely lead to another round of pain for me.

In my desperation, I convinced myself that it was a positive development. It was time to get over Kayla once and for all. I tried to recall all of the things that made us incompatible. She rose at the crack of dawn, unlike yours truly; she had children who might not accept me; she was a cat person, while I was a dog person; and most of all, she valued being on her own. She had often expressed her preference to remain single.

On my solo drive home that Sunday, I reviewed our weekend together. Kayla had shown no change toward me. We were wonderful friends who shared a common spiritual path – period. Having met her family, I better understood the challenges they faced, and I could be even more supportive. Prior to that visit, the full reality of her brother's and father's health issues had not registered with me. Both of them had advanced cancer.

I assumed that the visit was a significant step in our friendship. She shared more of her life with me, and I was not going to abuse that trust.

I had known for a long time that Kayla was a teacher of unconditional love for me. Whenever we were together, I was filled with a warm sense of being where I belonged. I loved her, and that love only grew with our shared experiences. It became easy for us to share what was going on in our lives.

Kayla fit my vision of a soulmate. I had come to believe that such people can be in our lives as friends, lovers, family members or colleagues. More often than not, soulmates are not intimate partners. I had accepted – and had done my best to appreciate – that Kayla and I had shared other times and places together, but would not be lovers in this lifetime, regardless of my strong feelings for her.

I was concerned that over the weekend, she might have picked up on my emotions and would therefore feel compelled to put distance between us. Gathering up my courage, I invited Kayla out for dinner the following week. On the drive back from the restaurant, I shared the feelings that I had experienced during my visit to her family home.

My goal was to confirm that our friendship took precedence over any romantic feelings that I might have for her. I admitted to having had a wonderful time with her family, and that the visit had stirred up old emotions. I assured her I was content with nothing more than her friendship. As I finished my mini-monologue, I told her that I would be the first person to be happy for her if she ever found a partner. I added that I hoped that he and I might be friends.

It took a few moments for her to respond. My only desire was that she would reaffirm our wonderful relationship. Instead, she asked, "What if that partner is you?"

My heart skipped a beat. I was incapable of responding; it was the last thing I had expected.

I do not know which one of us was more surprised by her response – that is still up for debate. She gave me a sheepish look, as if to say, "Where did that come from?"

"Kayla, are you sure?"

"No, I am not sure of anything right now."

"Well, I am sure that I love you. You've known this for a long time. If you are willing to explore us being together, I would be delighted. For my sanity, we need to make a decision one way or the other. I can be your friend, or I can be your partner, but I cannot be left wondering."

She nodded that she understood.

We sat in her driveway for a few minutes, each quietly considering what to do next. Finally, I broke the awkward silence.

"I have a number of things I need to do tomorrow. Please sleep on what just happened, and let's get together two days from now. I want us to decide then once and for all what we are going to do. Are you OK with this?'

"I think so. I love you, but I am terribly confused," she admitted.

"That's understandable. I gather that neither of us expected this. I will love you no matter what; but as I said, it is time to decide."

The next day passed in a blur. I was busy with activities to close out my career, and yet I longed to call her to find out how she was feeling. Resisting that overpowering urge – knights are good at that – I headed for her home on Tuesday. She greeted me at her kitchen door and we hugged. We then sat down at her kitchen table.

Not knowing how to start the conversation, I asked, "How are you feeling?'

"I have been a mess and my emotions are all over the place," she said, as tears began to form in her eyes.

I was feeling lost. My heart was ready to jump out of my chest. Here was the woman I longed to be with; yet, the idea of possibly having a relationship with me seemed to be causing her emotional anguish. Unsure of what to say, I reached over, took her hand, and placed it on my heart. From somewhere inside of me, words spilled out:

"Do what is in your heart. If you do, everything will be OK."

Somehow, those words touched something inside her. She got up and sat on my lap. With tears streaming down her face, she kissed me. It was our first real kiss.

From that moment, my life shifted direction. Even though the Knight in me had experienced many lifetimes, he could still be surprised – again.

Summer

Twilight of the Knight

From that first kiss, Kayla and I were inseparable. We somehow skipped the entire dating phase; we went from close friendship to full-on intimate relationship in an instant. Maybe having known each other for a decade and having communicated our respective trials and tribulations to each other had a lot to do with it. I sure did not need any time to ponder what I wanted – it was her, pure and simple.

Before we got together, I had already arranged to drive to San Antonio to pick up a new car that I had purchased. Why was I driving all the way out to Texas for a vehicle? It is because I wanted a small wagon with a manual transmission. I still enjoyed the engagement of a manual and it wasn't lost on me that driving one possibly saved me from a serious accident. VW still offered one at that time, and there were only two such cars that I could locate east of the Rockies. Unfortunately, the closer one, in Florida, was black. I did not want the car in black, so I decided to make the trip to San Antonio for the other one, which was white. I also planned to hand off my then-current car to a friend who was flying in from California. My itinerary also included time with friends in Houston.

It was heartrending to leave Kayla behind. On several levels, the trip turned out to be different from others in recent memory. It started with extreme weather variations. At first, the rain was so heavy that I had to drive at less than 30 mph. Later, I would be cruising along beneath sunny skies. What surprised me was how many times the weather on my trip cycled in and out of such disparate conditions.

I did not know how much the rapidly-changing weather would foreshadow the events to come.

During the drive, Kayla called to tell me she was leaving for her family's home. She said that her dad, Michael, was in the hospital. His cancer had abruptly accelerated, and on top of that, he had pneumonia. The prognosis was not good.

By the time I arrived in Houston, I found out that he was in intensive care and hospice was in charge of his case. I asked Kayla if I should be on the next available flight to join her; her answer was a simple, "Yes."

I was on a flight that evening, arriving at 11 p.m. Kayla picked me up, and we headed to the hospital. Because her dad was heavily sedated, he did not consciously know we were there. I took a seat at the end of the bed.

I did my best during the quiet hours of the night to connect with his spirit and to help him make an easy transition. I wordlessly communicated with him, and told him how much his family loved him. I described the multitude of souls I saw awaiting him; there were family members, friends and pets there.

The rest of the night passed in a blurry haze. I had an overwhelming sense of sadness; I was already missing a man I hardly knew. Michael departed into spirit the next day in a peaceful transition.

Two nights later, around 3 a.m., Kayla woke me. She was having a panic attack. She was shaking and had a look in her eyes like she would like to run somewhere – if only she knew where.

We spent the rest of the night examining the fear she was experiencing. As we delved into the role that fear was playing in both of our lives, insights emerged. We realized that much of her fear was not actually hers. Instead, she carried fears and concerns for others; doing so was part of her self-defined role.

Part of her identity was based on shouldering burdens for others. If she loved someone, she wanted to lessen their load. While a noble quality, it really does not serve either person well. When we carry others' burdens, it does not allow anyone to move forward. Kayla and I realized that we both had a propensity to take on the burdens of others.

What we discovered would shed light on the warrior essence within us. For me, the willingness to share others' burdens was an aspect of my identity, encompassed within the Knight. As we closely examined the role that fear played in our lives, we came to a startling conclusion. Our finding arose from the simple question: "How does fear serve us?"

For most of us, fear is an unpleasant feeling; yet, we continue to recreate it. If we view ourselves – on any level – as warriors or protectors, then fear has a central role. Without the threat of fear, what heroic role is there for the warrior or knight?

My Knight's purpose in my past lives was to fight against evil, and to protect those who could not protect themselves. With no evil to fear and fight against, what would have been my Knight's purpose? I could see that the fears I experienced throughout many lifetimes allowed me to hold on to that part of my Knight's identity. Without Kayla's help, I may never have gained such an understanding.

But what about threats that are real, in the present day? As Kayla and I considered that point, we realized two significant things. What happens to us is not as important as how we respond to what is happening. We can experience fear and internalize it, or we can see the hidden lessons. The law of attraction says we will validate and perpetuate what we hold inside. Therefore, emotions – like fear and guilt – have tremendous power to create our reality. The world conforms to our strongest feelings and beliefs. We then build our identities in response to our unique views.

Kayla and I decided it was time to stop feeding our warrior aspects and to let go of the fear that had been a cornerstone in our lives. So, the next evening, we went out to the porch and prepared to take another step forward in our transformations. The warm night air flowed through the porch screens and the tree frogs were in full voice. I had forgotten how noisy the nights can be when you are out in the woods. However, the vociferous pulse of nature was a fitting backdrop as we sought to change our own natures.

After getting comfortable, we spent a few minutes discussing what we planned to do, and in what sequence. Before focusing on our fears, we began with prayer. We asked that we be allowed to carry only our own burdens and to allow others to carry theirs. We felt lighter, and ready for whatever was next.

We decided to tackle the fear in two steps. First, we would focus on releasing the need for fear to justify our warrior and protector identities. Next, we would actually let go of our identities as warriors or protectors.

I remember little of what happened during the first step, except that I felt something deep within me shift and relax. Then, something more dramatic happened.

The Sword is before me. I am holding it chest-high, parallel to the ground; my arms are outstretched, palms facing upward. The Sword's handle is in my right hand. The blade's flat side rests in my left hand. Watching the sword, it changes from a weapon of war made of the finest steel to densely-packed particles of light. Its density shifts as I witness its disintegration. My hands are empty. I am filled with the Sword's pure love energy.

My identity as a Knight had gone through a complete transformation since my Ultimate Quest began. The Knight was my touchstone as I came to better understand myself as a spiritual being. When he first appeared, my Knight felt betrayed and angry, and he carried the mantle of failure. He had willingly given up his life because he saw no other alternative – all that he had held sacred led him to slaughter and disillusionment.

The Knight's emergence in Year One sent me on a journey of discovery that I could not have imagined. The visions he gave me – including death and destruction transforming into fields of flowers – and the message he conveyed propelled me forward on my uncertain Quest.

My Knight was transformed into a prince who held the Sword. In some ways, I was being brought back, full circle, to those first two workshops in North Carolina and Canada where the Quest's adventures began.

When I think of the Sword, there is still a reverence that grips me. I feel it in my chest. The immense energy that flowed through the Sword when it first appeared removed all thoughts that my life would be normal. On the outside, I had a career, a home, and a dog – all the things that go along with a regular life. But on the inside, I was transforming – driven by far more questions than answers.

Eventually, the Sword returned to its true essence of pure love, and that transformation signaled the end of the warrior within me – the one who took life. I was instead awakening to the incredible power of love that lives within all of us – the pure love that fosters life, compassion and joy.

A Reason, a Season, a Lifetime

I gained more than I could imagine from being with Kayla – first as her friend for more than a decade, and then as her partner. She shared her family and her pets with me (I learned that I could love cats as much as dogs) and the place she came from. Thanks to her, we moved to a community that included a supportive interfaith group and wonderful neighbors. I was also shown how people can live together in a way that I did not know was possible.

This new community also brought a chance for me to work with two nonprofit organizations that broadened my idea of service to others. Kayla was, and is, one of my teachers when it comes to unconditional love – and for that, I am forever grateful.

There is a saying: "People come into your life for a reason, a season, or a lifetime." Many people are not meant to be with us forever, even when we want them to be. Moreover, sometimes – despite our best efforts – love affairs with unlimited potential end.

In all the "normal" aspects of life, such as politics, spirituality, children, and finances, Kayla and I made a wonderful team. It was in our more subtle shadow-sides that we found that happiness could not thrive. After seven years as partners, we ended our relationship. I am sure that we are not unique in having such an experience. However, and more significantly, I believe we created opportunities for each other to embody unconditional love.

YEAR FIVE
Looking Back

Through Year Five of my Quest, I led two distinct lives: the spiritual and the professional. That was about to change. My Quest had changed me to the point that I could not continue as I had for so many years.

At that time, if someone had asked me what I most desired in my career, I would have said to be awarded a professorship or an endowed chair. Either honor would have been a wonderful recognition of a successful academic career. And, during Year Five, I was offered a professorship while I was on partial leave. Accepting the offer would have meant a nice salary increase and would have provided discretionary research funds. The offer was, in many ways, a dream come true after working so hard throughout my career.

Being on partial leave meant that I could continue to work with my colleagues and my doctoral students, but I was released from day-to-day teaching and my committee assignments. I knew that if I accepted the professorship, I would be required to return to full-time duties.

I felt that a lot had unfolded since the Knight appeared to me and changed my life back in Year One.

I was at a decision point. My academic pursuits seemed less important to me than discovering more about myself and what I was meant to accomplish.

I asked myself some key questions. *Can I walk away from my career – the one I have invested so much of my life and identity in for 30 years? Should I turn down something I have worked for over my entire career?*

As the deadline to decide approached, I thought about the different aspects of my job as a full-time academic. *Do I want to return to teaching?* I asked myself. The answer was: *Not really.* For one thing, the classroom experience was evolving and becoming more technology-based, and I was finding it more difficult to relate to the students and their world.

I thought, *Do I want to initiate new research projects and begin working with new doctoral students?* Again: *Not really.* The data we had collected on organizational change, spanning 10 years and involving thousands of employees, had yielded wonderful results. What we learned was summarized in our book, *Change the Way You Lead Change.* The book and the research that led up to it felt like a fitting conclusion to my academic life.

And with the professorship, there would be more administrative duties. *Is this the direction I want to go?* As much as I taught about managing and leading, I had no desire to direct my fellow academics.

But there was the critical question of finances. Was I in a position to retire on the money I had saved, and what income could I receive from other sources? In retrospect, I should have analyzed my projected expenses and income in detail in order to determine my best choice.

But I did not. Here, I took a leap of faith. You see, throughout my life, I had lived below my means. My recreational activities of bicycling and sea kayaking did not involve significant expenses, and my material desires had always been modest. I concluded that I would never starve.

My leap of faith also involved knowing that there were things for me to do, such as writing this book and the one on unconditional love. I realized that having a defined job – although it was something that had served me well for many years – would now be an impediment. By this point in my life, I no longer had two clearly separate professional and spiritual lives. They had merged.

I decided that I would continue writing, as I had done throughout my career, but now it would be about spiritual journeys and unconditional love. My Quest had bestowed so many significant gifts upon me; now, it would be time to share them with the world. Every challenge I would face in my transition to "retirement" would be an opportunity to grow.

So, in the later part of Year Five, I submitted my retirement letter. My decision shocked many of my colleagues, who could not imagine me passing up the professorship. Some of them probably could not believe that their workaholic colleague had much of a life outside of academia. The professorship would have been wonderful; but in the end, there were other things for me to do.

Any regrets? NONE!

The Gifts of the Quest

The Gifts

So, what does all of this mean? In the end, my Ultimate Quest bestowed many valuable gifts upon me, in the form of universal lessons. I would like to share them here, in hopes that they will enrich and ease your own spiritual journey.

There is a Pony in There Somewhere!

There is a saying that goes, "With all this manure, there must be a pony in there somewhere." Much of what life dishes up can appear to be manure – one struggle or challenge after another. But we can remind ourselves that there is, indeed, a pony in there.

On some level, we set in motion what we experience. We choose how much we learn from the world, which is a mirror for us. I know that the learning experience can be hard, but the more we accept that challenges can bring knowledge, the easier it becomes.

My Knight rejected a world that did not – and would never – conform to his beliefs. He chose death instead. But death did not end the struggle or bring him peace;

it only delayed what he needed to face. He reemerged in me to learn the lessons that eluded him in the past.

Many spiritual traditions teach that our greatest difficulties are also our greatest opportunities. We can be gardeners who use the manure to grow flowers and fruit that bring beauty and sustenance – to our lives and to the world. When I am struggling, I have adopted a shortened version of that philosophy: "I know there is a pony here somewhere."

In my darker moments, I remind myself that I can rise – like the phoenix – from the ashes of pain. For example, there were many lessons that came from my Judas role. The gifts from that life-changing experience turned out to be invaluable. In the case of my Judas experience, there was more than one pony. It seems that the more challenging the lesson, the greater the potential gifts.

Finding the Pony

It can be impossible to find the pony if we blame others for what is happening in our lives. Most of us play the victim at times; probably more often than we realize. We explain our unpleasant feelings and responses in terms of external influences – they are caused by what is happening to us. For instance, when we are sick, we say it is because a disease attacked us.

Are we victims, or is it possible that we select and attract events so we can grow? Many spiritual traditions suggest that we are an expression of the Divine; then, how can we be victims? As I consider that question, I recall the many lifetimes that I discovered during my search to understand the Knight. I also think about the gifts that each lifetime brought to me. If we cycle in and out of earthly experiences in order to evolve into true emanations of love, are we ever victims?

Neale Donald Walsch *(Conversations With God)* and Dan Millman *(Way of the Peaceful Warrior)* both say that our experiences are opportunities to move forward in our quests to heal and grow. Placing blame on others, or on outside forces, for what is occurring in our lives only pushes away chances for healing and expansion.

Love Is the One True Protection

My Knight believed that his armor, shield, sword and training kept him safe. Ultimately, they did not. What brought about his end on that battlefield was the pain that resided inside. The pain of feeling betrayed, the pain of believing he had lived a lie, and then the most devastating pain – the knowledge that his life and sword were dedicated to causing others' suffering. His pain then grew to the point where he could no longer stand it. What I have come to realize from my Quest is that pain resides and grows where love is absent.

The episode involving my Judas role was a perfect example of how the absence of love brought pain. Kimberly did her best to shield herself from what she believed were my attacks. Yet, from what she told me, her efforts were not effective. And when she requested help from her mentor, Kimberly was asked what she needed to heal. Her mentor explained that we are vulnerable in all areas where we are not holding love.

My role as Judas illuminated so many things that I needed to heal, and showed me where I needed to bring love. Where I held anger and fear, I experienced tremendous pain.

In modern times, we talk about people "pushing our buttons." When our buttons are pushed, we can experience anger and frustration. But once we bring love and understanding to those buttons, the pain goes away. Those buttons are no longer connected to our emotions and we have healed another part of ourselves. We have also taken another step toward being our authentic self, which is the whole point of the Quest. Love is the ultimate protection and the only protection. All other forms of protection eventually fail.

The Knight's True Quest Is for Unconditional Love

Dan Millman also said that the spiritual warrior's real sword is pure love. It brings forth life, not destruction. It clears the way for us to know the journey to that love.

My Knight's Quest is to embody unconditional love. Love – while ubiquitous in thought, words, and song – is difficult to pinpoint and possibly even harder to practice. Most of us have only experienced conditional versions of love from others and ourselves. Even the gods that mankind has worshiped – at least, according to tradition and scripture – are often judgmental, and their love and acceptance of humanity depends on what we do and how we do it. If the gods we have prayed to for centuries are not good role models, where do we turn?

Knights have the tendency to take on foolish tasks, and therefore I figured that a better understanding of unconditional love would be a fitting challenge for my Knight. I believe that there are three important points that we should focus on while on the path to unconditional love – acceptance, gratitude and forgiveness.

Acceptance Is the Antidote

Feeling unworthy may be a part of being human, but it keeps us from love. The Knight in me never believed himself worthy of God's love. He did not realize that love was already inside of him, and so he kept trying to earn love by chasing perfection – even when that meant killing others. He felt as if he could never perform enough acts of bravery or valor to receive God's love.

The answer to our feelings of unworthiness is acceptance – acceptance of both the good and the bad in ourselves. Accepting ourselves allows us to accept others. Can we accept things we see as negative or evil? Can we embrace the light, the dark, and the shadow? A friend of mine had been striving to earn Source's love. However, she felt inadequate because she knew she was not perfect. As I listened to her describing her imperfections, the message I received from Source was, "I have **no desire** for you to be perfect, so why should you?" As I relayed that message to her, I felt some of my own anxiety subside.

Adopt an Attitude of Gratitude

It is easy to be grateful for the blessings in our lives, but it is more challenging to also be grateful for the tough times. I understand why we have to tolerate the dark times, but it is another thing to appreciate them. The Knight in shining armor had trouble with that. But often, what appears as negative or tragic in the beginning can end up being a blessing. The serious bicycle accident

I had in the 1970s, which I mentioned in the introduction, was just such an experience for me.

It was a perfect June morning, and I was enjoying my brand-new bike on a group training ride. We were preparing for amateur racing. As we crossed over a bridge, my front wheel dropped into a gap, jammed, and pitched me straight down toward the pavement.

After I regained consciousness, I felt a burning sensation on the left side of my face. My face was damaged; X-rays showed a flattened cheekbone. A few days later, I was on an operating table. Ironically, that accident changed the course of my life, and opened up a whole new world for me.

The time I spent convalescing in the hospital gave me the opportunity to reassess my life. I was also able to be present at my grandfather's passing. The way I see it now, the accident led to: a meditation practice to lessen the migraines that resulted from the crash; a more rewarding career; a changed view of death and dying; and a mark on my face that has been a conversation-starter with countless strangers. The way I understand it now, the accident was a wakeup call that kicked off a series of events for which I am most grateful. However, since then, I have tried to find less painful ways to grow.

Forgiveness Is Freedom

Letting go of thoughts that connect us in negative ways to individuals, groups, events or memories is so important because what we do not forgive remains with us. Holding a grudge is like running a race while dragging an anchor. What we do not forgive stays in our shadow, and will influence our thoughts, feelings and actions. My Knight spent lifetimes holding onto fear, anger and unforgiveness. Those negative emotions prevented acceptance and gratitude.

When we can forgive ourselves and the realities we have created, we will emerge from our cocoons to the reality of love. Love is the only enduring reality and forgiveness is the key.

If you would like to journey deeper into unconditional love, I have dedicated an entire book to the topic – *Awaken to Unconditional Love: New Wisdom From 20 Spiritual Masters* (O'Leary Publishing, 2021).

The Key to the Quest

By now, you might be wondering – were my experiences with the Knight, Sword, Stallion, Archangel Michael, etc., real, symbolic, or purely delusional? I suggest to you that the answer does not matter. Much like life-changing spiritual experiences reported in books like the Bible, and like those occurring to many of us every day, they were real to me. Similar revelations and insight can change the direction of your life, too.

My hope is that *The Ultimate Quest* will help you to discover the truth of who you are and the power of love that you hold within you. Earth can be a challenging place, but our greatest answers emanate from the Source within each of us. We are the true authors of the quests we experience each and every day. We hold the keys to our own unique spiritual journeys.

Do your best to be loving and courageous. During the dark times, join me in looking for the pony. And know, without a doubt, that you are not alone. With that, I wish you, dear readers, love, joy and peace.

The Knight in me salutes you!

The Ultimate Quest

There is my tale, it is not so unique;
Go on your journey to find what you seek.

We've come to this life with purposes galore;
To heal, to serve, to lead and so much more.

Sometimes your journey will feel a complete mess;
Let love be your guide, its path who can guess?

Turn toward the light and ask for the way;
Opportunities will come for you each day.

Heed the call of your heart's deepest desire;
Its love will take you higher and higher.

The path of love is not easy, as foretold by many;
You cannot count on being paid, not even a penny.

Do it just because it is what you've come to do;
To the Light, Spirit, Source, and thy self be true.

ACKNOWLEDGMENTS

Authors often state that while the book they wrote is of their creation, they could not have done it without significant contributions of time and effort from others. This is especially true for this book. While written from my perspective, this book encompasses the journeys of many others as well.

Except for well-known figures, such as Wayne Dyer, the names of those who were involved in my journey were changed. While I did my best to protect their identities, they know who they are, and that I am forever grateful to them. My hope is that I contributed to their lives as they contributed to mine.

My heartfelt gratitude goes out to Joanne Tailele, who did the initial editing on this book. I also want to express appreciation to April O'Leary and Heather Davis Desrocher (Founder/Publisher and Head Editor, O'Leary Publishing, respectively) and their wonderful team, including Boris Boland (Line Editor), Kat Langenheim (Copy Editor), and Jessica Angerstein (Book

Designer), who all worked patiently with me. It was a team effort in the creation of a book that I am proud to share.

Many others, including Valerie Johnston, Karen Coratelli-Smith, Susan Ellison, Jack Fedor, Dorothy Fedor, William Anderson, Linda Walker, Debra Ting, Bob and Sue Ramsay, Mary Reining, Gail Elizabeth Altschwager, James Brophy, Janeen Dishman, Patty Meyers, Julie Ellis, Donna Lee, Shawn Williams, Birgit Blecken, Karen Beard and Richard Kurzenberger, were kind enough to read drafts and provide invaluable comments.

Thank you, all!

FOOTNOTES

1. What I used to clear the vows was Vianna Stibal's ThetaHealing™. It is based on the healing power of love. She calls the source of that love, The Creator of All That Is. The technique allows for the removal of those beliefs we no longer want to hold and enables us to replace them with what we desire. For example, we can remove a vow of poverty and replace it with the Creator's definition of abundance, including what it feels like to live in abundance.

2. Applied kinesiology (AK), also known as muscle testing, is based on the principle that we can get to underlying beliefs in our subconscious via our body, bypassing our conscious mind. AK begins by establishing how our body provides "yes" or "no" responses to statements of belief, whether they are true or false. There are a number of ways to perform AK, but a common way is for the subject to stand erect with the dominant arm extended directly out from the side of the body parallel to the ground. With the

help of someone else, the person being tested would resist that person pushing down on the outstretched hand. Saying a firm "yes" usually strengthens us, so for most people, a "yes" response (either verbally or as a thought) to a true statement would allow the arm to strongly resist being pushed down. On the other hand, thinking or saying a definite "no" usually causes a weakness in the arm and would allow it to be pushed down. The same level of strength would not be there.

For example, if you want to find out if you totally love and accept yourself, you can say, "I completely love and accept myself," and see how your body responds. The challenge is to allow the answer to come from within and not override it with our conscious mind, which, in this case, might think, "Of course I love and accept myself." For details and more complete treatment of different AK methods, you can check Frost and Goodheart (2013), *Applied Kinesiology, Revised Edition: A Training Manual and Reference Book of Basic Principles and Practices,* or Charles (2019), *Journey to Healing: The Art and Science of Applied Kinesiology.*

READINGS AND REFERENCES

A Course in Miracles (2004). Glen Ellen, CA: Foundation for Inner Peace.

Byrne, R. (2006). *The Secret*. New York, New York: Atria Books.

Charles, E. (2019). *Journey to Healing: The Art and Science of Applied Kinesiology*. Melville, New York: Renaissance Publishers.

Ford, D. (1999). *The Dark Side of the Light Chasers*. New York, New York: Riverhead Books.

Freston, K. (2006). *The One: Discovering the Secrets of Soul Mate Love*, Miramax Books, New York.

Frost, R. and Goodheart, G. (2013). *Applied Kinesiology*, revised edition: A training manual and reference book of basic principles and practices. Berkeley, California: North Atlantic Books.

Gibran, K. (1923). *The Prophet*. Alfred A. Knopf, Inc.: New York, New York.

Gilbert, E. (2006). *Eat, Pray, Love: One Woman's Search for Everything Across Italy, India, and Indonesia*. New York, New York: Penguin Group.

Green, G. (1999). *Love Without End: Jesus Speaks*. Fort Worth, TX: Heartwings Publishing.

Ingerman, S. (2008). *Shamanic Journeying: A Beginner's Guide*. Boulder, Colorado: Sound True, Inc.

LaBay, M.L. (2004). *Past Life Regression: A Guide for Practitioners*. Trafford Publishing: Victoria, BC, Canada.

Liaros, C.A. (2003). *Intuition Made Easy*. Cloudbank Creations: Corvallis, Oregon.

Millman, D. (1984). *The Way of the Peaceful Warrior*. H.J. Kramer: Tiburon, California.

Renard, G. (2004). *The Disappearance of the Universe: Straight Talk About Illusions, Past Lives, Religion, Sex, Politics, and the Miracle of Forgiveness*. Carlsbad, California: Hay House, Inc.

Stibal, V. (2007). *ThetaHealing*. Rolling Thunder Press.

Walsch, N.D. (2005). *The Complete Conversations with God: An Uncommon Dialogue* (containing books 1, 2, and 3). New York, New York: G.P. Putnam's Sons.

BOOK GROUP DISCUSSION QUESTIONS

1. What was your overall impression of the book?
2. Did you find it engaging, challenging, disconcerting, or ...?
3. Have you had similar experiences to the ones that occurred in the book? If so, which one was your turning point, like the appearance of the Knight was to Don Fedor?
4. If you could meet with Don Fedor, what questions would you ask him?
5. In what ways did the Ultimate Quest touch your emotions and feelings?
6. Could you relate to Don's dilemma when he believed he was causing harm to others in his spiritual group?
7. Do you have a different view of love, now that you have read the book?
8. Do you have a personal Quest? How did you come to learn about it?

ABOUT THE AUTHOR

Don Fedor is Professor Emeritus, Georgia Institute of Technology, Atlanta, Georgia. He received his PhD from the University of Illinois, Champaign-Urbana, his MBA from the University of Denver, and his bachelor's degree from Bucknell University. During his academic career, he published in business and psychology research journals, co-edited a research series, and co-authored the book, *Change the Way You Lead Change* (Stanford University Press, 2008) with David M. Herold.

Don is a Theta Healing Practitioner and a Healer Member of NFSH – The Healing Trust (UK). He is a student of *A Course in Miracles,* and longtime member of Edgar Cayce's Association for Research and Enlightenment (A.R.E.).

Don is the author of *Awaken to Unconditional Love: New Wisdom From 20 Spiritual Masters* (O'Leary Publishing, 2021). You can reach him with comments or questions at his Facebook page (Don Fedor), or by going to @donfedorphd on Instagram.

www.ingramcontent.com/pod-product-compliance
Lightning Source LLC
Chambersburg PA
CBHW050314120526
44592CB00014B/1907